Writing Papers
in Psychology

Writing Papers in Psychology

A Student Guide

Second Edition

Ralph L. Rosnow
Temple University

Mimi Rosnow

Wadsworth Publishing Company
Belmont, California
A Division of Wadsworth, Inc.

Psychology Editor: *Ken King*

Editorial Assistant: *Cynthia Campbell*

Production Editor: *Carol Carreon*

Managing Designer: *Carolyn Deacy*

Print Buyer: *Barbara Britton*

Permissions Editor: *Peggy Meehan*

Cover and Interior Design: *Michael Rogondino*

Compositor: *Rogondino & Associates*

Copy Editor: *Steve Bailey*

Technical Illustrator: *Pat Rogondino*

Cover Photograph: © *Stuart Simons, 1990*

Signing Representative: *Joyce Larcom*

Printer: *Malloy Lithographing*

1 2 3 4 5 6 7 8 9 10—96 95 94 93 92

ISBN 0-534-16986-4

Library of Congress Cataloging-in-Publication Data

Rosnow, Ralph L.
    Writing papers in psychology : a student guide / Ralph L. Rosnow,
Mimi Rosnow. -- 2nd ed.
        p. cm.
    Includes index.
    ISBN 0-534-16986-4 (alk. paper)
    1. Psychology--Authorship. 2. Report writing. I. Rosnow, Mimi,
1938- . II. Title.
BF76.7.R67 1992
808'.06615--dc20   91-18881

To the partnership that brought this book about

Ralph L. Rosnow
is Thaddeus Bolton Professor of Psychology
at Temple University

Mimi Rosnow
is an editorial assistant at a national magazine

Contents

Preface

This manual speaks to undergraduate students in psychology who are looking for a resource and guide to walk them through the steps used in writing a term paper or a research report. In an age where television pictures and the spoken word seem to prevail, the written word has a unique, indeed almost old-fashioned, power to compel, persuade, and convince—that is, to communicate ideas. We hope this manual will ease the process of communicating ideas effectively and also will leave the student with the profound sense of satisfaction that we associate with effective written communication.

The information presented is applicable to both the term paper and the research report except for Chapters 3 and 4, which focus on each topic in turn. We contrast the two forms and explain the way in which a student proceeds step by step from beginning to end: choosing a topic, using the library, structuring the paper, writing and polishing it, and producing the final manuscript. We do not discuss the technical criteria of good scientific hypotheses (falsifiability, parsimony, and cohesiveness, etc.), because we assume that the student assigned to write a research report is being taught this information with the aid of a research-methods text. Although we present many style tips, we assume that the student already has been exposed to basic writing techniques. If basic skills need polishing, we recommend that the student read William Strunk, Jr., and E. B. White's *The Elements of Style* (3rd ed.). We did not want to burden psychology students with a manual so technical and detailed that it could serve as a textbook in a writing course.

Guided by the following flow chart, most students should be able to master this manual in a few hours; they can then refer to specific chapters and sections as needed:

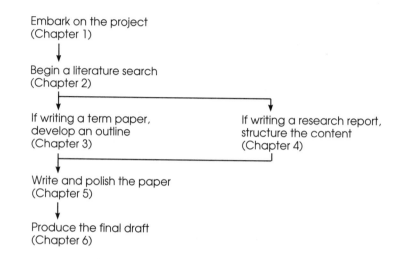

Embark on the project
(Chapter 1)

Begin a literature search
(Chapter 2)

If writing a term paper, develop an outline (Chapter 3)

If writing a research report, structure the content (Chapter 4)

Write and polish the paper
(Chapter 5)

Produce the final draft
(Chapter 6)

Comments on the Second Edition

Instructors who are familiar with the first edition will recognize several refinements in this new edition. For example, the discussion of how to conduct a literature search has been expanded by the addition of a section on PsycLIT. This section also includes guidelines that were developed and tested by Donna Shires, a teaching fellow at Temple University. Another addition is the expanded discussion of plagiarism, which includes a specific example and advice on how to avoid this problem. Helpful pointers on the use of word processors are interpolated throughout the manual. Also new is the background information on browsing in the library's stacks to encourage serendipity.

We have moved the recommended style closer to that specified in the *Publication Manual of the American Psychological Association* (3rd ed.), but continue to encourage a commonsensical, problem-solving approach to style. We are not sticklers for stringent professional guidelines for students who are fulfilling a course requirement and have no wish to submit their papers to a psychological journal. For example, the APA Manual's rule for submitting articles for publication is to place tables and figures at the end of the manuscript. We recommend a simplified format for in-text placement of tables and figures that makes the paper easier to read. We also recommend that the research report contain an appendix for raw data, calculations, lengthy questionnaires, and so on.

Acknowledgments

We thank Maria (Di Medio) Mastrippolito and John Yost for giving us permission to edit their work and include the edited versions as sample presentations. We thank Mary Lu Rosenthal for counseling us through two editions of this manual on the methods and means of conducting a successful literature search in a modern college library. We thank Donna Shires for allowing us to incorporate her suggestions on how to use PsycLIT. We thank a long line of graduate teaching fellows and undergraduate students at Temple University and Harvard University for their valuable comments and criticisms of this manual's first edition. We thank the following Wadsworth consultants for their constructive feedback during various phases in the development of the first and second editions: John B. Best, Eastern Illinois University; David Goldstein, Duke University; James W. Kalat, North Carolina State University; Allan J. Kimmel, Fitchburgh State College; Joann Montepare, Tufts University; Edgar O'Neal, Tulane University; Robert Rosenthal, Harvard University; Gordon W. Russell, University of Lethbridge and John Sparrow, SUNY, Geneseo. The first author also acknowledges the support he has received from Temple University in the form of the Bolton Professorship. Finally, we both thank Ken King for his helpful suggestions and unflagging support.

For students and others who desire a comprehensive guide to preparing an article for publication in a journal that uses the APA format, there is no substitute for the APA Publication Manual. Although that was not the audience we had in mind in writing this manual, we found the APA Manual to be enormously useful in reminding us of technical points we might have forgotten to mention. We advise students to seek the latest edition available and thus avoid consulting outdated sources. For this reason, we do not always specify publication dates for books mentioned in this text. Among the other manuals that also were helpful were: R. Barrass, *Scientists Must Write* (Wiley, 1978); R. W. Bly and G. Blake, *Technical Writing: Structure, Standard, and Style* (McGraw-Hill, 1982); B. L. Ellis, *How to Write Themes and Term Papers* (Barron's, 1989); D. E. Fear, *Technical Writing* (Random House, 1973); H. R. Fowler,

The Little, Brown Handbook (Little, Brown, 1983); J. Gibaldi and W. S. Achtert, *MLA Handbook for Writers of Research Papers* (Modern Language Association, 1988); K. W. Houp and T. E. Pearsall, *Reporting Technical Information* (Macmillan, 1984); C. Hult and J. Harris, *A Writer's Introduction to Word Processing* (Wadsworth, 1987); M. H. Markel, *Technical Writing: Situations and Strategies* (St. Martin's, 1984); M. McCormick, *The New York Times Guide to Reference Materials* (Dorset, 1985); D. J. D. Mulkerne and D. J. D. Mulkerne, Jr., *The Term Paper* (Anchor/Doubleday, 1983); L. A. Olsen and T. N. Huchin, *Principles of Communication for Science and Technology* (McGraw-Hill, 1957); J. G. Reed and P. M. Baxter, *Library Use: A Handbook for Psychology* (American Psychological Association, 1983); B. Spatt, *Writing from Sources* (St. Martin's, 1987); K. L. Turabian, *A Manual for Writers of Term Papers, Theses, and Dissertations* (University of Chicago, 1955); and J. E. Warriner, *Handbook of English* (Harcourt, Brace, 1951).

R.L.R.
M.R.

Writing Papers
in Psychology

1

Getting Started

The term paper and the research report are distinctly different forms that share certain similarities. Both have a relatively simple format; both are written for a specific reader, the instructor; and both require that the steps in the project be paced so that the assignment, completed on time, represents your best work. This chapter focuses on the rudiments of getting started: that is, helping you know where you are heading and formulating a plan to get you there on schedule.

Know Your Objective

Before you turn on a word processor or begin to sharpen any pencils, ask yourself this question:

Do I understand the assignment?

If you are not *sure* of the answer, ask the instructor what is expected of you. You can talk with other students to get their impressions, but the instructor is the only person who can describe the assignment accurately. Most instructors find that one student in every class goes off on a tangent and then suffers the consequences of a low grade. Don't let that student be you!

Here is a checklist of questions that you might ask yourself before proceeding:

- What is the objective of the writing assignment?
- Do I choose the theme or topic, or will it be assigned by the instructor?
- How long should the paper be?
- Will progress reports be required? If so, when?
- When is the final report due?

A sense of the differences between the term paper and the research report (see Exhibit 1), will help you focus your efforts on whichever form you have been assigned.

One distinction highlighted in Exhibit 1's table is that a literature search usually will form the core of the term paper, while data form the core of the research report. The literature search for the research report usually involves only a few key studies to serve as a theoretical starting point, so you can expect to spend a lot more time in the library if you are writing a term paper. Of course, you still must spend time in the library if you are writing a research report, because you will need to look up background information.

A second distinction shown in the table is that the structure of the term paper, although somewhat formal, is more flexible than that of the research report, which has a more standardized structure. Term papers are relatively flexible because there are different

Exhibit 1   Differences Between Term Papers and Research Reports

Term Paper	Research Report
1. Based on literature search; no hard data of your own to interpret	1. Based on data that you have collected; literature search involving only a few key studies
2. Structured by you to fit your particular topic	2. Standardized structure
3. Puts ideas into a context of a particular thesis	3. Reports your own research findings to others

types that represent widely different objectives. Most instructors expect the structure of the research report to conform to the general form specified in the *Publication Manual of the American Psychological Association* (APA Manual). That is, the research report will contain an abstract, an introduction, a method section, and so forth.

The final distinction noted in Exhibit 1 is that the term paper puts issues and ideas into the context of a particular theme or thesis, whereas the objective of the research report is to describe your research findings to others. We will have more to say about this last point later.

Three Types of Term Papers

There are three basic types of term papers—expository, argumentative, and descriptive—and each has its own objective.

First, the **expository term paper** is illustrated by Maria Di Medio's essay in Appendix A (page 75). The word *expository* means "to expound," "set forth," or "explain," and its purpose is to inform the reader on a specific subject or theme—in Maria's case, on treatments for anorexia nervosa. Such papers call for simplicity in writing, like the articles that are in the science section of *The New York Times* each Tuesday. Maria does not begin by writing, "I am going to explain how anorexia nervosa is treated." That is, in fact, her aim (implicit in the title of her paper), but her opening sentence is more polished and inviting.

Second, the **argumentative term paper** is intended to persuade the reader. For example, you might write an essay asserting the superior cost-effectiveness of behavior therapy as opposed to some other psychotherapeutic approach, or you might write a paper that argues for the applicability of cognitive dissonance theory in a realm beyond that for which it was originally intended. This type of paper asks readers to change their minds on a particular issue. As in any fair argument, all viewpoints should be represented and not just in a "take it or leave it" fashion. Show that you recognize gray areas as you develop your position and present significant documentation to support it. If you are arguing against a particular viewpoint, collect specific quotations to show that you have represented the opposing view accurately. Otherwise, you may be accused of making a "straw man" argument, which means that you have represented the other side in a false, unfair, or misleading way to buttress your personal view. It can be helpful to argue one's point of view with someone who is a good listener and promises to be very critical; jot down that person's questions and counterarguments while they are fresh in your mind so that you can deal with them in your paper.

Third, the purpose of the **descriptive term paper** is to map out its subject, to express how things are. Examples might include a case study involving some personal experience or a narrative interpretation of a particular event. If you were writing a descriptive essay in an English course, it would be an opportunity to exercise your creative ability. Creativity also is valued in science, but when describing things you want to be accurate and not take a flight of fancy. An effective descriptive essay in psychology will not be vague, but will incorporate specific examples and faithful quotations to support ideas.

Incidentally, whichever type you have been assigned to write, most term papers are 10 to 20 pages long. Maria's paper in Appendix A illustrates the recommended format of an expository paper, although not necessarily its recommended length.

Three Types of Research Reports

Researchers make fine distinctions between the various kinds of research approaches (for example, the laboratory experiment, the field experiment, the sample survey approach, the case study), but it is convenient to boil them down to three general types—descriptive, relational, and experimental. The structure of the research report will be similar in each case, but the objective of the report will be different.

First, the purpose of the **descriptive research report** (like the descriptive term paper) will be to map out its subject. For example, you might report the observations you made of first-year students thrown together for the first time as roommates in a dormitory. Another illustration of descriptive research would be a psychologist who was interested in studying children's failure in school. The researcher might begin by spending a good deal of time observing the classroom behavior of children who are doing poorly. The researcher then would describe what was observed as carefully as possible. Careful description of failing pupils might lead to ideas about how to revise our concepts of classroom failure, to suggestions of factors that may have contributed to the development of failure, and perhaps to innovative hypotheses concerning the remediation of failure.

The careful description of behavior is a necessary first step in the development of a program of research. Sooner or later, however, someone will want to know *how* what happens behaviorally is related to other variables. That is the objective of the **relational research report,** which examines the way in which events are related or the way behavior is correlated with another variable. For instance, you might report on how college students behave differently toward one another over time; time would be one variable, and behavior would be the related variable. In Appendix B, John Yost's report (page 88) is an example of relational research. John examines the difference in people's confidence in rumors and how such a difference is correlated with rumor transmission. The researcher interested in failure in school might note for each pupil (a) whether that child was learning anything or the degree to which the child had been learning and (b) the degree to which the teacher had been exposing the child to material to be learned. The finished report then would examine the relationship between the amount of pupils' exposure to material to be learned and the amount of such material they in fact did learn.

Third is the **experimental research report.** We learned that descriptive reports examine *how things are* and that relational reports examine *how things are in relation to other things.* The purpose of the experimental report is to examine *how things get to be the way they are.* For example, you might report on how social behavior in rats is affected when the experimenter manipulates the animals' reinforcement schedules. In the case of children's failure, the researcher might examine whether teachers actually teach less to pupils whom they believe to be less capable of learning. In the finished report, the researcher would concentrate on the question "What leads to what?" in the situation of pupil failure as a function of teachers' expectations of such failure.

Scheduling Time

In his autobiography *The Shaping of a Behaviorist* (New York University Press, 1984), psychologist B. F. Skinner recollected how he had sought to discipline himself by developing a very strict regimen when he entered Harvard University as a graduate student in 1928:

> I had done what was expected of me in high school and college but had seldom worked hard. Aware that I was far behind in a

new field, I now set up a rigorous schedule and maintained it for almost two years. I would rise at six, study until breakfast, go to classes, laboratories, and libraries with no more than fifteen minutes unscheduled during the day, study until exactly nine o'clock at night and go to bed.

No one expects you to develop a schedule as stringent as Professor Skinner's when he was a student. However, once you feel that you know what is expected of you, it is time to set specific deadlines that you feel you can meet. You know your own energy level and thought patterns, so play to your own strengths. Are you a morning person? If so, block out time to work on your paper early in the day. Do you function better at night? Then use the late hours of quiet to your advantage. Allow extra time for other pursuits by picking realistic dates by which you can reasonably expect to complete each major part of your assignment. Write the dates on your calendar; many students also find it useful to post the dates over their desks as a daily reminder.

How do you know what tasks to schedule? If you look again at Maria's and John's papers in Appendixes A and B, you will see that writing a term paper calls for a different schedule than writing a research report. As we said, writing a term paper requires spending a lot of time in the library accumulating source materials, so you will need to leave ample time for that task. Here are some hints about what to schedule in your calendar:

- Completion of outline of term paper
- Completion of library work
- Completion of first draft of term paper
- Completion of revised draft(s) of term paper
- Completion of final draft of term paper

If you are assigned a research report, set aside ample time for these major tasks:

- Completion of proposal for research
- Completion of data collection
- Completion of data analysis
- Completion of first draft of research report
- Completion of revised draft(s) of research report
- Completion of final draft of research report

By scheduling your time in this way, you will not feel pressured by imaginary deadlines or surprised as the real deadline approaches. Get started right away—do not procrastinate. Organizing, writing, and revising will take time. Library research does not always go smoothly; a needed book or journal article might be unavailable. Data collection and analysis also can run into snags: Research subjects might not cooperate or a computer might be down.

If you get started early, you also will have time to write to authors for unpublished or follow-up manuscripts if you think you need them. (Students often are surprised to learn that they actually can write to an author of a research study and ask about the author's most recent work.) If you want to use a published test or questionnaire in your research, you need to give yourself time to locate a copy and (maybe) get permission to use the instrument.

Note that both schedules of tasks allow time between the first and final drafts to distance yourself from your writing. This allows you to return to your project with a fresh perspective as you polish the first draft and check for errors in logic, flow, spelling, punctuation, and grammar. Another word of advice: Instructors have heard all the excuses for a late or badly done paper, so do not expect much sympathy if you miss the final deadline.

Choosing a Topic

The selection of a suitable topic is an integral part of learning, because usually you are free to explore experiences, observations, and ideas to help you focus on specific topics that will sustain your curiosity and interest as you work on your project. In considering a suitable topic, beware of a few pitfalls; the following are "dos" and "don'ts" that might make your life easier as you start choosing a topic:

- Be enthusiastic and strive for a positive attitude.
- Use the indexes and tables of contents of standard textbooks as well as class notes for initial leads or ideas you would like to explore more fully.
- Choose a topic that piques your curiosity.
- Make sure your topic can be covered in the available time and the assigned number of pages.
- Don't be afraid to ask your instructor for suggestions.

- Don't choose a topic that you know other students have chosen; you will be competing with them for access to the library's source material—as well as for a good grade.

Shaping the Topic

Choosing too broad or too narrow a topic for a term paper or research report surely will add difficulties and also will mean an unsatisfactory result. A term paper that is too broad—for example, "Freud's Life and Times"—would try to cover too much material within the limited framework of the assignment and the time available to complete it. A specific aspect of Freud's life and times would prove a more appropriately narrowed focus for treatment in a term paper.

However, in narrowing the topic, do not limit your discussion to facts that already are well known. There are two simple guidelines:

- Be sure that your topic is not so narrow that reference materials will be hard to find.
- Be guided by your instructor's advice.

If you approach instructors with several concrete ideas, usually you will find them glad to help tailor those ideas so that you, the topic, and the project format are compatible.

Here are examples of how you might shape the topic about Sigmund Freud by a specific working title:

Unlimited topic (much too broad)

"Life and Times of Sigmund Freud"

Slightly limited topic (still too broad)

"Psychological Theories of Sigmund Freud"

Limited to 20-page paper

"Freud's Theory of Personality Applied to Mental Health"

Limited to 10-page paper

"Freud's Theory of Infantile Sexuality"

Too narrow a topic

"Freud's Pets"

You can always polish the title later, once you have finished your library search and have a better sense of the topic.

Here is another example of shaping a topic. This time the assignment is a research project, and the student must choose a topic in an area of social psychology:

Unlimited topic (too broad for a term project)

"Who Gossips and Why?"

Slightly limited topic (still too broad)

"When Do People Gossip?"

Adequately limited topic

"Content Analysis of Selected Gossip Columns Over a Specified Period"

Know Your Audience and Topic

Professional writers know that they are writing for particular audiences. This knowledge helps them determine the tone and style of their work. Think of a journalist's report of a house fire and contrast it with a short story describing the same event. Knowing your audience is no less important when the writer is a college student and the project is a term paper or a research report. The audience is your instructor. Should you have questions about the instructor's standards and expectations, then find out what they are before you set to work.

For example, in a research-methods course taught by one instructor, the students were told that the grading criteria for different parts of the finished report would be as follows:

Introduction (20 points)
clarity of purpose (10)
literature review (10)

Method (20 points)
   adequacy of design (10)
   quality and completeness of description (10)
Results (30 points)
   appropriateness of analysis (5)
   correctness of analysis (10)
   use of tables or figures (5)
   clarity of presentation (10)
Discussion (20 points)
   interpretation of results (10)
   critique/future directions (10)
Miscellaneous (10 points)
   organization, style, etc. (5)
   appendix (5)

This kind of information enabled the students to concentrate on different parts of the assignment in the way that the instructor would concentrate when critiquing their reports.

This information also can serve as a checklist for you to ensure that everything of importance is covered adequately in your finished report. Not every instructor will provide such detailed information about grading, but this manual can help you compose your own refined checklist.

Let us assume that you know your audience—your instructor. Now you must cultivate more than just a superficial understanding of your topic. The more you read about it and discuss your ideas with friends, the more you will begin to develop an intuitive understanding of the topic. We have three suggestions:

- Many writers find it helpful to keep several 3x5-inch index cards handy to jot down relevant ideas that suddenly occur to them. This is a good way to keep your subject squarely in your mind.

- You also must comprehend your source material, so equip yourself with a good desk dictionary and turn to it routinely whenever you come across an unfamiliar word.

- While you shop for a dictionary, you also might buy a thesaurus. It can be useful as an index of terms in information retrieval as well as a treasury of synonyms and antonyms when you write.

2

Using the Library

Knowing about the many resources available in the library and knowing how to use them will prove invaluable to you. Familiarity with the many recent technological advances in library research can help save time and effort. This chapter will tell you about traditional and innovative resources to help you use the library most effectively.

Plan of the Library

If you have not set foot in your college library, then begin by familiarizing yourself with the floor plan to find out where the major sections are. You can ask at the information desk whether there is a fact sheet that describes where to find things. You also can make your own fact sheet as you take an orientation tour. It is inconvenient to return to the information desk every time you have a question, so be aware of other places you can turn to for assistance. Usually, library staff members (often called *information librarians*) also are available at the reference desk and the catalog desk. Each area provides specialized help in orienting library users to the resources at hand. Do not be afraid to ask for guidance. Information librarians derive personal and professional satisfaction from being helpful and informative.

Here is a quick summary of what you can expect to find at each location:

- *Information desk.* This is a general assistance area—the name speaks for itself. The staff members at this desk will refer you to the appropriate section of the library to find particular source material or to the appropriate librarian who can answer specific questions. While you are here, find out what days and hours the library is open.

- *Reference desk.* Staff members at this desk are true generalists who can either answer all manner of questions or point you to sources that will help you answer them yourself. They may, for example, suggest general reference works such as *Psychological Abstracts* or *Social Sciences Citation Index.* Because this material is "not circulated" (not available to be checked out), you will have to work within a specified section of the library. If your library has a machine-readable data-base system (such as PsycINFO or PsycLIT), then ask the reference librarian for information about the use of this resource, including its cost.

- *Catalog desk.* This is the heart of the library; the card catalog file usually is located nearby. The staff members at this desk can provide assistance on how to use the card catalog as well as how to use a computer to access this information—that is, if you have any questions after reading this chapter.

How Material Is Cataloged

There are two easy ways to search for what is available in the library: by using either the card catalog or a computerized system if one is available. The card catalog is another name for the miles and miles of index cards that appear in alphabetical order in file drawers. The computer system is a user-friendly, menu-driven, automated data base that provides public access to the same information by having you key in the answers to simple questions shown on the screen.

Some computer systems are designed specifically for a given library (such as Harvard University's HOLLIS, which is quite a good automated catalog), and some are generic designs sold by vendors. Some of these systems leave a lot to be desired, but most college and community libraries are trying to replace the card catalog with a computerized system, particularly for their current acquisitions. And these automated systems do make it easier for both patrons and library staff members, who must maintain the catalog. The simplest way to find out just how easy it is to use the computerized system is by trying it.

As noted, the card catalog (on which the computerized system is based) is a file of alphabetized 3x5-inch cards. The cards tell us what is in the library and where to find it. Some libraries list periodicals (journals, magazines, newspapers) separately in a serials catalog—frequently in a book or microfilm format of alphabetized listings.

Suppose you wanted to check out a book by Robert Rosenthal and Lenore Jacobson titled *Pygmalion in the Classroom*. The library's books usually are entered on three types of catalog cards: (a) author cards, (b) title cards, and (c) subject cards. If you looked in the card file under either "Rosenthal, Robert" or "Jacobson, Lenore" (author card) or *"Pygmalion in the Classroom"* (title card), you would find a **call number** indicating where this book is stored in the library stacks (the shelves throughout the library). The stacks are coded according to categories that coincide with the numbers and letters on the index card in the card catalog and the image on the computer screen. To help us locate the right book, the call number also appears at the bottom of the book's spine.

The author card for Rosenthal and Jacobson's *Pygmalion in the Classroom* is shown in Exhibit 2. The information in the upper-left corner is the call number—a sequence of letters and numbers specified by the Library of Congress to identify this work.

With few exceptions, each item held by the library (textbooks, reference works, phonograph records, disks and tapes, VCR and

Exhibit 2 Sample Catalog Card

LB	**Rosenthal, Robert,** 1933—
1131	Pygmalion in the classroom; teacher expectation and pupils'
R585	intellectual development [by] Robert Rosenthal [and] Lenore
	Jacobson. New York, Holt, Rinehart and Winston [1968]
	xi, 240 p. illus. 23 cm
	Bibliography: p. 219–229.

1. Prediction of scholastic success. 2. Mental tests. I. Jacobson, Lenore, joint author. II. Title.

LB1131.R585   372.1'2'644   68–19667

Library of Congress

motion-picture films, and so on) has a catalog card that gives a full description of the material and its call number. To find out whether your library has the book you are looking for, you need only the name of one author or the title of the work. Without such information, you also could search through the appropriate subject cards until you have located the work in question. (If you prefer to let your fingers do the walking, then let the computer access this information for you.)

Exhibit 3 shows the two systems of classification most frequently used in U.S. libraries. For psychology students these can be puzzling systems, because psychological material is classified under several different headings. The Library of Congress System divides material into 20 major groups; abnormal psychology books can be

Exhibit 3   Two Systems of Classification

Library of Congress System		**Dewey Decimal System**	
A	General works	000	General works
B	Philosophy and religion	100	Philosophy
C	General history	200	Religion
D	Foreign history	300	Social sciences
E–F	America	400	Language
G	Geography and anthropology	500	Natural sciences
H	Social sciences	600	Technology
J	Political science	700	Fine arts
K	Law	800	Literature
L	Education	900	History and geography
M	Music		
N	Fine arts		
P	Language and literature		
Q	Science		
R	Medicine		
S	Agriculture		
T	Technology		
U	Military science		
V	Naval science		
Z	Bibliography and library science		

found under either BF or RC. The Dewey Decimal System classifies material under 10 headings (and abnormal psychology can be found in the 157 class). If you are allowed to browse in the stacks, refer to Exhibit 4. It shows the cataloging of more specific areas by both systems. Browsing can be a way of discovering a valuable but unexpected book or a pungent quote to illustrate some idea or point.

Returning to Exhibit 2, the call number of Rosenthal and Jacobson's book tells us that we would first go to the LB section of the stacks and next to the more specific section in numeric (1131) and then alphanumeric order (R585) where this book is shelved. The card also shows the name and birth year of the first author (Rosenthal, Robert, 1933–). Below this is the title of the work and its subtitle *(Teacher Expectation and Pupils' Intellectual Development)*, followed by the complete list of authors in the order in which they appear on the title page of the work. Then follows the location and name of the publisher (New York, Holt, Rinehart and Winston) and the date of copyright (1968).

The remainder of the card lists further technical facts about this work for librarians. The information noted in the middle of the card shows the number of prefatory pages (xi) and the length of the book (240 p.); it also indicates that the book contains figures or other illustrations (illus.), that it stands 23 cm. high on the shelf, and that the bibliography is on pages 219 to 229. The section below that indicates the categories under which this book should be cataloged ("Mental tests," for example). Next is the book's Library of Congress classification number again (LB1131.R585), the Dewey Decimal classification number of this work (372.1'2'644), the order number of this particular set of cards (68–19667), and from whom the cards can be ordered (Library of Congress).

Doing a Literature Search

Let us explore some ways you might look for literature related to your project. You can do a hand search (which means you might take notes from a digest or compendium of abstracts), or you can use a machine-readable data base (which means a computer is used to access this information). The latter is easier and quicker, because it allows the user to combine certain subject terms and to exclude unwanted terms.

Exhibit 4   Cataloging of Psychological Materials

Library of Congress System		Dewey Decimal System	
BF	Abnormal psychology	00–	Artificial intelligence
	Child psychology	13–	Parapsychology
	Cognition	15–	Abnormal psychology
	Comparative psychology		Child psychology
	Environmental psychology		Cognitive psychology
	Motivation		Comparative psychology
	Parapsychology		Environmental psychology
	Perception		Industrial psychology
	Personality		Motivation
	Physiological psychology		Perception
	Psycholinguistics		Personality
	Psychological statistics		Physiological psychology
HF	Industrial psychology	30–	Family
	Personnel management		Psychology of women
HM	Social psychology		Social psychology
HQ	Family	37–	Educational psychology
	Psychology of women		Special education
LB	Educational psychology	40–	Psycholinguistics
LC	Special education	51–	Statistics
Q	Artificial intelligence	61–	Psychiatry
	Physiological psychology		Psychotherapy
QA	Mathematical statistics	65–	Personnel management
RC	Abnormal psychology		
	Psychiatry		
	Psychotherapy		
T	Personnel management		

Data-base systems use two basic approaches: the on-line and the compact disc. Besides the printed format of *Psychological Abstracts* (which we describe later), the abstract is available in both computer formats. The **on-line system** is called PsycINFO, and the **compact-disc system** is called PsycLIT. The advantage of the compact-disc format, as a librarian friend put it, is that users can search to their hearts' content, and librarians do not see all those dollar signs flying around in their heads (libraries, and ultimately users, must pay to access on-line services each time they are used; see Machine-Readable Data Bases, p. 21). As the name implies, the compact-disc format of *Psychological Abstracts* (PsycLIT) uses a removable disc to store information. Updated discs are supplied by the American Psychological Association on a quarterly basis to the library.

We will have more to say about PsycLIT later, but suppose all you need are four or five key citations to provide the basis for a working hypothesis in the introductory section of a research report. If you intend to do a hand search, a good place to look for key studies is the reference section or bibliography section of a standard textbook, source book, or annual review (such as *Annual Review of Psychology*). Another source of references on specific topics is the *Psychological Bulletin*, a journal of literature reviews; the last issue of every volume has an index. However, do not simply list citations of articles because your instructor will wonder if you have even read the study cited. **Read the original work.**

Most students do not find the literature search an onerous task, but some have the feeling that they are being asked to climb Mt. Everest without a Sherpa guide. If this describes you, then ask your instructor for some leads before you exhaust yourself searching aimlessly in the library for just the right reference or bibliography section. For example, the card in Exhibit 2 notes that this book contains an 11-page bibliography—surely a likely place to begin a search for key studies if you were writing a paper on the effects of teachers' expectations on pupils' behaviors. You then could track down four or five key works by comparing the reference sections of other books with this bibliography to find out what books or articles were cited by others. However, a much easier way to get this information would be to use the *Social Sciences Citation Index* (which we describe in a moment).

Suppose you were looking for a general reference work, an encyclopedia of psychology. There are, in fact, many such encyclopedias, including Benjamin B. Wolman's *International Encyclopedia of Psychiatry, Psychology, Psychoanalysis, and Neurology* (Van Nostrand Reinhold); Raymond J. Corsini's *Encyclopedia of Psychology* (Wiley); and H. J. Eysenck, W. Arnold, and R. Meili's *Encyclopedia of Psychology* (Herder and Herder). Other multivolume reference works that are relevant to psychology include *The Encyclopedia of Education* (Macmillan and Free Press) and *International Encyclopedia of Communications* (Oxford). Incidentally, if you happen to be looking for a reference book *about* reference books available in your field, ask an information librarian for E. P. Sheehy's *Guide to Reference Books.* This is a comprehensive, annotated listing of reference books; if you simply ask for "Sheehy's," the librarian will know what you mean.

Our librarian friend reminds us to emphasize that information librarians are highly skilled in helping students find material. No matter how much paperwork the librarian has on the desk and no matter how busy the librarian looks, students should not be intimidated. Do not be afraid to approach an information librarian for help, because that is the librarian's main purpose.

Indexes and Abstracts

Suppose you found a useful article or book that was published in 1968; its reference list sent you to related publications from 1968 and earlier. To find more recent publications on the topic, you could turn to the *Social Sciences Citation Index* (SSCI). This continuously updated series of volumes consists of three separate but related indexes to the behavioral and social science literature as far back as 1966. It shows—in alphabetical order by the authors' last names—the year's published literature that cited the work.

For example, if you looked up Rosenthal and Jacobson's *Pygmalion in the Classroom* in the 1984 SSCI, under Robert Rosenthal's name you would find the list of entries shown in Exhibit 5. Each entry is a work that refers to this book (for example, Anderson, K. M.), the source of the work (*Elementary School Journal*), the volume number (84), the beginning page number (315), and the year of publication (1984). You then can go to the periodicals section of your library and examine the references to see whether they are pertinent to your work. A companion index, the *Science Citation Index* (SCI), also lists citations of works not usually

Exhibit 5 SSCI Citations of *Pygmalion in the Classroom* in 1984

68 PYGMALION CLASSROOM		VOL	PG	YR
ANDERSON KM	ELEM SCH J	84	315	84
BALL DW	PSYCHOL REP	54	347	84
BLANCK PD	J EDUC PSYC	76	418	84
BROPHY J	CC/SOC BEH		16	84
BUGENTAL DB	MON S RES C	49	1	84
CADMAN D	AM J PUB HE	74	1093	84
CARROLL JL	PSYCHOL SCH	21	343	84
COLVIN M	AM J SOCIOL	89	513	83
COOPER HM	ELEM SCH J	85	77	84
CORSON D	"	84	458	84
EDEN D	ACAD MGMT R	9	64	84
EHRENWAL J	J AM S PSYC	78	29	84
ERWIN PG	BR J ED PSY	54	223	84
GRIM P	NEW IDEAS PS	2	35	84
HENDRICK I	J AS STUD P	18	3	83
KARPER WB	EDUC RES Q	8	40	83
LEMIRE G	CAN J CRIM	26	459	84
MARSHALL HH	REV EDUC RE	54	301	84
MARTIN DS	J REHABIL D	17	17	84
MARTINEK TJ	J SPORT PSY	6	408	84
"	RES Q EXERC	55	32	84
MCGOWAN RJ	HISPAN J B	6	205	84
MCWHIRTE JJ	PERS GUID J	62	580	84
MOULDEN M	ENVIR PLA	16	49	84
PROCTOR CP	ELEM SCH J	84	469	84
RAMPAUL WE	ALBER J EDU	30	213	84
RAUDENBU SW	J EDUC PSYC	76	85	84
RICHEY LS	J LEARN DI	16	610	83
ROSENTHA R	J CONS CLIN	52	679	84
SAFRAN SP	LEARN DISAB	7	102	84
SCHWARZW J	MEGAMOT	28	207	84
SMEAD VS	ALBER J EDU	30	145	84
STRYKER S	ADV EXP SOC	16	181	83
SWANN WB	J PERS SOC	46	1267	84
"	PSYCHOL REV	91	457	84
TSUI AS	ORGAN BEH H	34	64	84
WATSON W	SOCIAL SC M	19	629	84

Exhibit 6 Sample Abstracts from *Psychological Abstracts**

13800. **Baumrind, Diana.** (U California, Inst of Human Development, Berkeley) **Specious causal attributions in the social sciences: The reformulated stepping-stone theory of heroin use as exemplar.**
Journal of Personality & Social Psychology, 1983(Dec), Vol 45(6), 1289–1298.
—Examines the claims based on causal models employing either statistical or experimental controls. Such claims were found to be excessive when applied to social or behavioral science data. An exemplary case, in which strong causal claims are made on the basis of a weak version of the regularity model of cause, is critiqued. J. A. O'Donnell and R. R. Clayton (see PA, Vol 70:12937) claim that to establish that marihuana use is a cause of heroin use (their "reformulated stepping-stone" hypothesis), it is necessary and sufficient to demonstrate that marihuana use precedes heroin use and that the statistically significant association between use of the 2 drugs does not vanish when the effects of other variables deemed to be prior to both of them are removed. Here, it is argued that O'Donnell and Clayton's version of the regularity model is not sufficient to establish cause and that the planning of social interventions both presumes and requires a generative rather than a regularity causal model. Causal modeling using statistical controls is of value when it compels the investigator to make explicit and to justify a causal explanation but not when it is offered as a substitute for a generative analysis of causal connection. (41 ref)—*Journal abstract.*

14246. **Searcy, William A.** (U Pittsburgh) **Response to multiple song types in male song sparrows and field sparrows.**
Animal Behavior, 1983(Aug), Vol 31(3), 948–949.
—Examined whether J. R. Kreb's (1977) hypothesis, which proposes that song repertoires in birds function in territorial defense, can explain interspecific differences in repertoire size. 30 male field sparrows (*Spizella pursilla*) and 30 male song sparrows (*Melospiza melodia*) were tested. Contrary to predictions, male field sparrows, which lack repertoires, showed a preferential response to multiple song types, while male song sparrows, which possess repertoires, did not. It is concluded that Kreb's hypothesis does not explain the interspecific difference in repertoire size in these sparrows. (7 ref)

15519. **Berndt de Souza Mello, Jansy. Dois triângulos. [Two triangles.]**
(Port) *Alter-Jornal de Estudos Psicodinâmicos,* 1980(Jan–Dec), Vol 10(1–3), 77–82.
—Relationships in the Oedipus myth can be seen as a triangle of father, mother, and child, one member being excluded from the opposite pair. The present author contends that the psychoanalyst–patient relationship can be thought of as a triangle formed by the patient, the patient's memories and emotions, and the analyst with his/her outside perspective. In the transference relationship the analyst may be included in the patient's memories. An analyst, excluding him/herself may interrupt the patient to aid progress to a more human and realistic relationship. In a clinical example, a patient simultaneously addresses an analyst both as a real person and, in the transference relationship, as a loved one. (English abstract) (4 ref)—*G. L. Chesnut.*

14747 **Epstein, Joyce L.** (Johns Hopkins U, Ctr for Social Organization of Schools) **Choice of friends over the life span: Developmental and environmental influences.**
Center for Social Organization of Schools Report, Johns Hopkins U., 1983(Jul), Rpt No 345, 96 p.
—Presents a life-course perspective on the selection of friends. Research results on 3 aspects of the selection process are discussed: (1) facts of selection—the number of friends and their proximity; (2) the surface of selection—the visible features of friends such as their sex, race, and age; and (3) the depth of selection—characteristics of friendships and similarity of friends. Over 250 references are reviewed to learn how patterns of selection change with age and under different environmental conditions from preschool to post-secondary school settings. The research reveals important developmental patterns in the selection of friends. With age and with the development of cognitive skills and experiences, older students tend to choose fewer best friends, make choices from wider boundaries, increase cross-sex choices, decrease cross-race choices, move toward mixed-age choices, reciprocate and stabilize friendships, and choose more similar friends. There are also important environmental effects on choice of friends. For example, elementary, junior high, and high schools may be organized to encourage wide or narrow contacts; to reward, ignore, or punish cross-sex, cross-race, or mixed-age choices of friends; or to emphasize differences or similarities among students. These and other environmental conditions affect selection in ways that revise expected patterns of choosing friends. Ideas for new research are presented that stress the importance of developmental and environmental factors in studies of friendship selection and influence. (15 ref)—*Journal abstract.*

indexed in the SSCI. But some works are listed in both the SCI and SSCI, so it may pay you to check them both.

Psychological Abstracts, on which PsycLIT is based, gives synopses of thousands of works in psychology and related disciplines. Exhibit 6 shows a sample of the wide range of works available in this resource, including four abstracts from a volume of *Psychological Abstracts* published in 1984 (volume 71): (a) an article criticizing another article, (b) a theoretical paper in a foreign journal, (c) a research study on animal behavior, and (d) a literature review. Each abstract contains information about the particular work.

For instance, Baumrind's abstract begins with a *Psychological Abstracts* code number (13800), so you can easily find the abstract again by going back to this volume and looking up this code number. The author's name then is listed; if there were more than four authors, the first author would be listed and followed by "et al." The first author's affiliation is given next, and then the work's title is shown, followed by the journal (or other) source in which the work appeared. If the work is written in a foreign language (as in the abstract of Berndt de Souza Mello's work in Portuguese), then the original title would be followed by the translated title. A synopsis of the work follows; next are the number of references and the source of the abstract.

Other useful abstracts in psychology and education include *Sociological Abstracts* (1952 to present), *ERIC* (Education Resources Information Center), and the often overlooked *Social Sciences Index* (1974 to present). There are abstracts and indexes for just about every discipline and area of interest (e.g., *Biological Abstracts, Art Index, Abridged Index Medicus, Humanities Index*), and an information librarian will be glad to direct you to the relevant indexes and abstracts. *Psychological Abstracts* (and most other indexes) include an author index and a subject index. The subject index can be valuable if used with care. Avoid looking up a broad topic that will have pages of listings; for instance, to find material on learning abilities of insects, check *insects*, not *learning*.

Machine-Readable Data Bases

The term **machine-readable data base** is computer jargon that means the file of information sought is accessible by means of a video screen or a computer printout. A computer search is usually faster and more fun than a hand search, and using a machine is really the only way to begin an exhaustive search on a given topic. In some libraries this service is free; others charge.

If your library does the search for you, then begin by talking with a librarian who can help you choose correct key words and descriptors to facilitate your retrieval of the desired literature and to exclude scores of irrelevant citations. You will be asked to pare down your topic as precisely as you can and to avoid undertaking a complete search on a broad topic. For example, if you ask for on-line material on "social behavior in children," you may get an unmanageable printout and a big bill. Like painting a room or blacktopping a driveway, the more effort and thought spent in conscientious preparation for the task, the better the final outcome.

Be prepared to consider the following points when you approach the librarian to place your on-line order:

- What is the particular topic to be searched? In answering this question, use special terms as well as common words, including synonyms and alternate spellings. Answer the question as fully as possible, and define any words or phrases you use that may have special meaning within your area of interest.

- Describe any related terms or applications in which you are not interested so that the computer can be instructed to discard seemingly relevant but actually inappropriate references. Your answer to this question will help reduce the cost of your on-line search. One resource to help you pare down the search is the American Psychological Association's *Thesaurus of Psychological Index Terms*.

- List two or three of the most important authors on your topic. This, plus the following three points, will help the computer zero in on your topic.

- List two or three of the most important journals in your subject.

- List two or three of the most significant articles on your topic. If you do not know enough about your subject to do this, ask your instructor for suggestions or check recent source books or standard textbooks for clues.

- Give the time span that you would like the on-line search to cover. *Psychological Abstracts* covers the period from 1927 to the present, but PsycINFO (the on-line system) covers 1967 to the present and PsycLIT (the compact-disc system) covers 1974 to the present. The time spans of indexes and abstracts vary widely; the librarian will tell you the years covered by the data bases to which your library subscribes.

Using PsycLIT

If you are using PsycLIT, then you will find that it contains an on-screen tutorial to show you how to conduct a search. Press the "Ctrl" and "t" keys simultaneously and you will start up (boot) the tutorial. Once you have the PsycLIT system going, you can press the "F1" key to get any help you need. But you will find the system user-friendly and also time-saving if you do some homework on the topic before you actually get going. Looking in the *Thesaurus of Psychological Index Terms* can save you a lot of time and effort.

Donna Shires (of Temple University) recently had this to say about her experience using PsycLIT:

> I was writing a paper about how questionnaire results may be biased by the way the questions themselves are worded. Specifically, I was interested in the problem of people answering "yes" to questions that they might not really agree with. My understanding was that this problem was called "yea-saying." Armed with this limited knowledge, I got on PsycLIT and entered the term "yea-saying." I found only two articles which addressed this topic. Because my paper required a literature review, I became a little worried. Two articles could hardly be considered a literature review. At this point, I decided to go back to some textbooks that had information on questionnaire design. Upon reading more information, I discovered that the term "yea-saying" was not the most general or common term for the problem I was interested in. Rather, "acquiescent response bias," or some variation thereof, was the term of choice. When I got back on PsycLIT and plugged in "acquiescent," I found a whole list of articles. My literature review could proceed!

Donna ran into the opposite problem in another situation, when she turned up many articles that were not relevant to what she wanted:

> I was interested in finding studies that had looked at people's attitudes toward the mentally ill. I used the terms "attitude*" "mentally" and "ill" in this search. When I combined these (by first combining "mentally" and "ill" and then adding "attitude*"),

PsycLIT informed me that more than 70 articles contained these terms. In looking these articles over, I found that some had to do with attitudes *of* mentally ill people, not attitudes *about* mentally ill people. When I used the terms "mental" and "illness" with "attitude*" I located articles that dealt with attitudes *about* the mentally ill.

Donna prepares her own students with the following background information and hints:

- Actually using PsycLIT requires that you understand what it is capable of doing for you. It locates articles in psychology journals and journals in related fields. These articles are located based on the term(s) you tell PsycLIT to search for. At the "Find" prompt, you type in the term you want to use as the basis of your search. PsycLIT then will conduct a search, assign the search a number, tell you how many articles contain the term, and give you the option of looking at the citation and abstract for each article.

- The PsycLIT search process can be speeded up and simplified if you know a few "tricks." One is to search for only one term at a time. This means, generally, one word at a time. Let's say you want to find information on racial prejudice. The fastest way to do this search is by first typing in "racial" at the "Find" prompt. Once this search has been completed, tell PsycLIT to find "prejudice." Following this search, tell PsycLIT to find "#1 and #2" (or whatever the assigned numbers are). This approach works more efficiently than typing in "racial prejudice" as one term. Also, separating your search into specific words can save you time later. For example, let's say that you think that racial prejudice may be related to stereotyping. You do a search on "stereotype," which is assigned the number 5. You then can command PsycLIT to find "#1 and #5" to see what articles are available on racial stereotypes.

- How you spell the term you are searching for also is important. When searching the literature for articles on acquiescent responding, Donna found that some authors referred to this problem as "acquiescent response bias" and others used the term "acquiescence." Rather than conducting several searches using each variation, she typed "acquiescen*" at the "Find" prompt. In this way, she told PsycLIT to search for that particular term but allowed for several different endings to the term. Therefore, articles using both "acquiescent" and "acquiescence" came up in the search.

- The number of articles you locate can give you information on whether you are too narrow or too broad in your search. If your search locates no articles, then you probably are using the wrong term. If you only locate one or two articles, then you may be searching for something too specific or using the wrong term. If a search turns up large numbers of articles, then you may need to narrow your topic. One way is to add a term to narrow the search. For example, if you were interested in treatment of depression, you could specify particular types of treatment to get the number of articles down to a reasonable size. If you have your own personal computer with a floppy drive, then you can download information from PsycLIT and look it over at your convenience so large numbers of articles can be dealt with.

When it is time to print, download, or both, Donna prepares her students with the following hints:

- You will find it useful to have the complete abstract of the article as well as the citation. PsycLIT's default option is citation only, which then prints all articles located in the search. You will need to change "CITN" to "all" to get the full abstract.
- To get only specific articles, enter the code number assigned to these articles by PsycLIT. Articles are arranged chronologically; the most recently published are listed first.
- If you are printing out directly from the PsycLIT data base to a printer, then it generally is better to look over the articles and print only those that are relevant. This gives you more time to conduct searches, because most printers are not that fast.
- If downloading to a floppy disk, then you may just want to download all articles and look them over later. This saves the most time. However, make sure that you get the full abstract when you download, because the article citation alone tells you little.

Some Other Resources

Suppose you came across a word or phrase that you did not understand and could not find in your desk dictionary or in the library's unabridged dictionaries. If it was a psychological term, then you could try to find it in other reference works, such as the encyclopedias noted previously. The best unabridged dictionary of the English language is the multivolume *Oxford English Dictionary* (called the "OED"), which is fascinating to thumb through if you are interested in word origins. Its purpose is to give the history of all words in the English language from the year A.D. 1150 to the publication of the OED. There is an abridged edition in two volumes (also published by Oxford University Press), but you need a magnifying glass to read it. Some words in the OED have very different meanings today than they originally had, and it is interesting to learn about these changes in meaning. For an illustration, see Alexander Rysman's article in the 1977 *Journal of Communication* (Winter, pp. 176–180) on the history of the term *gossip*.

A great many other useful dictionaries and reference sources are available. For example, slang dictionaries will tell you the history of words such as *hot dog* and *meathead.* They also provide information on rhyming slang, black slang, pig latin, and so forth. If you are interested in information about people in the news, you can look in *Current Biography*. If you want to know about famous Americans past, then you can look in the *Dictionary of American Biography, Who Was Who in America: Historical Volume 1607–1896*, or *Who Was Who in America*. The *Dictionary of National Biography* tells about men and women in British history. An information librarian also can point you to other biographical works that you may find useful (e.g., *American Men and Women in Science* and *Who's Who In Frontier Science and Technology*).

Taking Notes in the Library

We have discussed locating material but said nothing about taking notes in the library. You need to take precise, carefully documented background notes to write an accurate paper. Detailed notes not only help you pull facts and ideas together into precise sentences and paragraphs but also help you avoid committing **plagiarism** accidentally. We will have more to say about plagiarism later, but you plagiarize intentionally when you knowingly copy or summarize someone's work without acknowledging that source. You plagiarize accidentally when you copy someone's work but forget to credit it or put it in quotes. Plagiarism is illegal, and you should guard against it when taking notes.

A good procedure for taking notes in the library is to use a separate index card for each quotable idea that you find as you uncover relevant material in your literature search. Many writers prefer making notes on 5x8-inch rather than 3x5-inch index cards, because they usually can get all the information they want on the front of a larger card, making it easier to find what they want later. Exhibit 7 shows two examples of notes taken for a term paper; the student has found two sections in one source for use in the paper.

Observe that the cards are numbered "1 of 2" and "2 of 2" in the upper-right corner, and the book's call number is included in the lower left. If you have made an outline for a term paper (as described in Chapter 3), you might code each card (in the lower right) with the particular section of the outline that the material on the card will illustrate. In this way you can maintain a general order in your notes and avoid facing a huge stack of miscellaneous bits and pieces of information that will loom large as you try to sort and integrate the information you find in the library into a useful form. Be consistent with all the reference numbers you use on your note cards; a haphazard arrangement will only slow you down when it is time to write the first draft.

These two cards contain a wealth of material. At the top of both is a complete citation. It will be required in your reference section (where you list all the sources you have cited) and will be condensed in the citations in the paper's narrative. The top card summarizes, in the notetaker's own words, the major details of the study reported by Rosenthal and Jacobson. This synopsis ends with a quotation chosen to illustrate Rosenthal and Jacobson's conclusions. Note that the page number of the quote is included, because the page number must be cited if the student decides to use this quote. On the bottom card the student has focused the material taken from this book by asking a particular question. The lengthy quotation copied from Rosenthal and Jacobson specifically addresses the question. Note that four dots (a period plus an ellipsis) interrupt the text halfway through the quote; they indicate that a portion of the quote has been purposely omitted by the student.

Additional Tips

Here are some more tips to help you get started on the literature search:

- Try to be realistic in assessing your literature needs. Too little work will result in a weak foundation for your project, but too much material and intemperate expectations can overwhelm you and your subject.

- How can you determine a happy medium between too little and too much? Talk with your instructor before you start an intensive literature search. Ask whether your plan seems realistic.

- Before you begin your literature search, ask the instructor to recommend any key works that you should read or consult. Even if you feel confident about your topic already, asking the instructor for specific leads could prevent you from going off on a tangent.

- Do not expect to finish your literature search in one sitting. Students with unrealistic expectations make themselves overly anxious and rush a task that should be done patiently and methodically to achieve the best result.

- In planning your schedule, give yourself ample time to do a thorough job. Patience will pay off by making you feel more confident that you understand your topic well.

- It is not always easy to discard a study that you have made an effort to track down, but quantity should not replace quality and relevance in the studies you finally use in your research report or term paper. Your instructor will be more impressed with a tightly reasoned paper than with one overflowing with superfluous background material.

- Suppose you cannot locate the original work that you are looking for in the stacks. Some students will return repeatedly to the library day after day seeking a book or journal article before discovering that it has been lost or stolen or is being rebound. Ask an information librarian to find the elusive material. If the original work you need is unavailable, then the librarian might consult another college library.

- If you are looking for a specialized work, then you probably will not find it in a small public library, so do not waste your time. When students spend a lot of time off campus in public libraries and bookstores looking for source material, they usually come back with references from general texts and current mass-market periodicals.

Exhibit 7   Sample Note Cards

---

1 of 2

Rosenthal, Robert, and Jacobson, Lenore (1968). <u>Pygmalion in the classroom:</u> <u>Teacher expectation and pupils' intellectual development.</u> New York: Holt, Rinehart and Winston

Teachers at "Oak School" (an elementary school in California) were led to believe that about 20% of students were potential "bloomers" based on their performance on a test to pick out intellectual bloomers (or spurters). Actually, the names of the 20% had been chosen at random and the test was a nonverbal IQ test (TOGA). All students were retested with TOGA after one semester, after a full academic year, and after two academic years. The IQ gains of the 20% (the experimental group) consistently surpassed the IQ gains of the remaining (control group) students. This result is consistent with Rosenthal's self-fulfilling prophecy hypothesis (see also Merton, R.). The authors conclude that "... one person's expectation for another person's behavior can quite unwittingly become a more accurate prediction simply for its having been made." (page vii)

LB1131.R585

---

2 of 2

Rosenthal, Robert, and Jacobson, Lenore (1968). <u>Pygmalion in the classroom:</u> <u>Teacher expectation and pupils' intellectual development.</u> New York: Holt, Rinehart and Winston.

What practical implications do these authors draw from their research findings? "As teacher-training institutions begin to teach the possibility that teachers' expectations of their pupils' performance may serve as self-fulfilling prophecies, there may be a new expectancy created. The new expectancy may be that children can learn more than had been believed possible, an expectation held by many educational theorists, though for quite different reasons .... The new expectancy, at the very least, will make it more difficult when they encounter the educationally disadvantaged for teachers to think, 'Well, after all, what can you expect?' The man on the street may be permitted his opinions and prophecies of the unkempt children loitering in a dreary schoolyard. The teacher in the schoolroom may need to learn that those same prophecies within her may be fulfilled; she is no casual passer-by. Perhaps Pygmalion in the classroom is more her role." (pp. 181-182)

LB1131.R585

Library Etiquette

Before we turn to the basics of outlining the term paper (Chapter 3) or structuring the research report (Chapter 4), here is some final advice when using the library. The golden rule of library etiquette is to treat others as you would have them treat you, which means:

- Be quiet while working in the library.
- Never tear out pages of journals or books.
- Never write in library journals and books.
- Do not monopolize material.
- Return books and periodicals as soon as you finish with them.

3

Outlining the Term Paper

Once you have chosen your topic and begun library work and note taking, the next step in developing the term paper is to make an outline. The imposition of form will help you collect and refine your thoughts as you shape the paper. (If you are writing a research report, then you can skip this chapter and go on to Chapter 4.)

Where to Start

Think of the outline as a road map to the ideas and notes that you are assembling to present in your paper. If done correctly, the outline will show a logical progression of the points of interest that the paper will cover. Initially, a tentative and general outline might be generated as you use the library's resources—a kind of shopping list for quotes and reference material that will serve to flesh out the paper when the time comes to sit down and write.

If you find it difficult to begin writing, you can try several tricks. One is to find a good quotation that can launch the introduction (called an **epigraph**) as well as capture and focus the reader's interest. A second trick is to ask yourself the reporter's questions: who, what, when, and why? A third trick is to use comparison and contrast as a way of structuring the outline in your mind; then collect specific facts and studies to document and expand on subtopics. Before you begin writing, however, you will want to revise the preliminary outline so that it reflects the organizational structure you will use to shape the paper.

Making Ideas Parallel

Outline items can be set down in three different forms, using topics, sentences, or paragraphs. The specific form chosen should be the only one used in the outline so that all the ideas are parallel. In the following outline fragment, based on Maria's paper in Appendix A, the ideas clearly are not parallel:

I. Nature of problem
   A. Food plentiful but eating disorder results
   B. How is it defined?
   C. Symptoms
      1. weight loss
      2. patient has a distorted body image
      3. amenorrhea
   D. Psychological aspects of the disorder include:
      1. perfectionist's disease
      2. see themselves as obese

The problem with this outline is that it is a hodgepodge of topics, idea fragments, questions, and so forth. Working with this jumble is like swimming upstream. Such an outline will only sabotage your efforts to put thoughts and notes into a logical sequence. Contrast this inconsistent structure with the parallel structure of the following outline as it covers the same points:

I. Nature of the problem
   A. Food plentiful, but eating disorder is widespread
   B. Definition
      1. *anorexia* from Greek "want of appetite"
      2. *nervosa* is a nervous condition
      3. a.n. defined by Dorland's (p. 94) as "a serious nervous condition in which the patient loses his appetite and systematically takes but little food, so that he becomes greatly emaciated"
   C. Physical symptoms
      1. loss of substantial body weight
      2. distorted body image
      3. possible presence of amenorrhea

   D. Psychological symptoms
       1. need for perfection
       2. distorted self-perception

Putting Ideas in Order

Whether you use topics, sentences, or paragraphs for your outline, group your information from the most general facts or ideas in descending order to the most specific details and examples. We see this clearly in the parallel format of the outline shown immediately above. As the following example illustrates, the same rule applies whether we are outlining definitions and symptoms or the nature of a specific therapeutic approach in a clinical investigation that we plan to develop further in the first draft:

   III. Weight gain–plus–therapy approaches
        A. Lucas, Duncan, & Piens (1976)
            1. separate anorectic from family
            2. institute weight-gain program
            3. use psychotherapy for patient
            4. use family therapy for patient's family
        B. Andersen (personal communication)
            1. begin nutritional restitution
            2. administer individual therapy
            3. give patient increased responsibilities
            4. use follow-ups to guard against relapse

Another rule is that there should be two or more subtopics under any topic, as illustrated in Exhibit 8. The use of roman numerals I, II, III; capitals A, B, C; arabic numerals 1, 2, 3; small letters a, b, c; and finally numbers and letters in parentheses serves as a means of classifying facts, ideas, and concepts. Thus if you list I, you should list II; if A, then B; if 1, then 2; and so on.

The roman numerals indicate the outline's main ideas. Indented capital letters provide main divisions within the groups of main ideas. The letters and numbers that follow list supporting details and examples. Note the indentation of each subtopic. Any category can be expanded to fit the number of supporting details or examples that you wish to cover in the paper. Any lapses in logic are bound to surface if this system of organization is used, so you can catch and correct them before proceeding.

Exhibit 8   Subdivision of the Outline

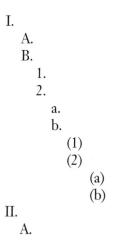

For example, look at the following abbreviated outline; the entry labeled "C" is a conspicuous lapse in logic:

I. Symptoms
   A. weight loss
   B. amenorrhea
   C. use psychotherapy for patient
   D. distorted body image

Item C should be moved from this section of the outline to that pertaining to therapeutic approaches. Another instance might require a return to the library to clarify a point or to fill in with the appropriate reference material.

Further Helpful Hints

The outline is a way not only to organize your thoughts but also to make it easier to start writing. With the phrase or sentence format, the paper will almost write itself. We see this clearly by returning to the outline of the opening section in Maria's paper:

I. Nature of the problem
   A. Food plentiful, but eating disorder is widespread
   B. Definition

1. *anorexia* from Greek "want of appetite"
2. *nervosa* is a nervous condition
3. a.n. defined by Dorland's (p. 94) as "a serious nervous condition in which the patient loses his appetite and systematically takes but little food, so that he becomes greatly emaciated"

Had the outline used complete sentences, the opening paragraph of Maria's paper would write itself:

I. Nature of the problem
   A. In a society where food is plentiful and a topic of obsessive attention, it is paradoxical that anorexia can be so prevalent.
     1. *Anorexia* is from the Greek "want of appetite."
     2. *Nervosa* indicates a nervous condition.
     3. Dorland's (p. 94) defines *anorexia nervosa* as "a serious nervous condition in which the patient loses his appetite and systematically takes but little food, so that he becomes greatly emaciated."
   B. Distorted self-image is one basic symptom, as victims starve themselves to achieve weight loss because they misperceive themselves as layered in fat.

In Chapter 2 we alluded to one other helpful hint about using an outline. The outline's coding system makes it convenient to code the notes you took during your literature search in the library. If the notes on an index card pertain to section "II.B.1." of your outline, then you would code this information on the card. In this way, order is brought to the stack of note cards that you have accumulated. If you spread them out on a table and sort them according to the section of the outline they pertain to, then the paper will take shape from your notes and the outline, each component enhancing the other.

Keep in mind, however, that the outline is only a guide. Its form probably will change as you integrate notes and outline.

Outlining After the Fact

Some people find the process of making an outline too exacting, preferring instead to sit at a word processor, typewriter, or with pencil and pad so that the stream of ideas can flow naturally. An experienced writer working with a familiar topic sometimes can achieve success with this unstructured approach. But for others, the results often can create havoc and frustration, not to mention wasted time and effort.

However, if you feel that you do not have the self-discipline to make an outline at the outset, at least make one later. To assure yourself that your work has a coherent form—what psychologists call a "good gestalt"—see if you can outline your first draft after the fact if you did not make an outline beforehand. Ask yourself:

- Is the discussion focused, and do the ideas flow from or build on one another?
- Is there ample development of each idea?
- Are there supporting details for each main idea discussed?
- Are the ideas balanced?
- Is the writing to the point or have I gone off on a tangent?

If you want to practice on someone else's work, try outlining Maria's term paper. Ask yourself how well her paper addresses the five preceding questions. If you discover problems with the structure of this paper, then think of ways she could have avoided or corrected them after the first draft.

4

Planning the Research Report

The research report has a structure in which data form its core. The literature review usually involves only a few key studies. This chapter describes the structure and form of the research report and suggests ways to begin organizing your thoughts. (If you are writing a term paper, then you can skip this chapter and go on to Chapter 5.)

The Basic Structure

By now, course work and your instructor's recommendations should have led you through the process of narrowing your area of interest so that your study is feasible and ethical and your methods and procedures are appropriate to it. Many research-methods texts routinely cover data-collection and data-analysis procedures. We will assume that you are mastering the relevant techniques they describe, so that all that remains is to plan a clear, concise report.

Notice that John's research report has eight parts:

- Title page
- Abstract
- Introduction
- Method
- Results
- Discussion

- References
- Appendix

Except for the layout of the title page and the addition of the appendix in this report, the structure corresponds generally to the standardized format recommended by the APA Manual. The title page is straightforward, so we will focus on the remaining seven parts of the research report.

Abstract

Although the abstract appears at the beginning of your report, it actually is written after you complete the rest of your paper. The abstract provides a concise summary of your report. Think of it as a distillation of the important points covered in the body of the report. Thus, in one succinct paragraph in the sample research report, John gives a synopsis of his hypothesis, the methodology of the investigation, and his results.

When planning your abstract, answer these questions as concisely as possible:

- What was the objective or purpose of my research study?
- What principal method did I use?
- Who were the research participants?
- What were my major findings?
- What can I conclude from these findings?

More detailed and more specific statements about methods, results, and conclusions are treated in the body of your report. The brief summary of the abstract lets the reader anticipate what your report is about.

Introduction

The introduction to the report should give a concise history and background of your topic. In the sample report, John has chosen to introduce his project by defining the term that forms the basis of his study and then describing the current status of the topic. In this way, the reader is given some general facts needed to appreciate and assess John's work. He cites specific studies to provide the reader with additional background on the topic and then raises a question

(Why are some rumors repeated more frequently than others?), which allows him to lead into his working hypothesis in an inviting way.

Generally speaking, the introduction provides the rationale for your study and prepares the reader for the methods that you chose to accomplish the research. The literature review shows the development of your working hypothesis and the reason you believe the research question to be important. The strongest introductions are those that describe the research problem or hypothesis in such a way that the method section appears to be a natural consequence of that statement. If you can get readers to think when they later see your method section, "Yes, of course, that's what this researcher had to do to answer this question," then you will have succeeded in writing a strong introduction.

Here are some questions to ask yourself as you plan this section:

- What was the purpose of my study?
- What terms need to be defined?
- How does my study build on or derive from other studies?
- What was my working hypothesis or expectation?

Method

The next step is to detail exactly the methods and procedures used. Care should be taken to describe fully the research participant pool: age, sex, and numbers of subjects, as well as the way in which they were selected and any other details that would help to specify them. Psychologists are trained to ask questions about the generalizability of research findings. Your psychology instructor will be thinking about the generalizability of your results across both persons and settings (i.e., the **external validity** of the results).

If you recruited participants from an available subject pool, then tell how many of the potential subjects actually volunteered. If you happen to know something about the characteristics of the subjects who did not volunteer (i.e., the nonrespondents), report this information as well (perhaps in a table that compares the characteristics of the respondents and nonrespondents). *The Volunteer Subject* (Wiley, 1975), by Robert Rosenthal and Ralph L. Rosnow, will help you explain the ways in which external validity may be affected by the subjects' volunteer status.

Also included in this section should be a description of the tests and measurements that you chose to use and the context in which they were presented. John's report describes the brief questionnaire that he prepared and the instructions given to the participants. He implies that subjects were assured of the confidentiality of their responses (because they were treated anonymously); generally it is believed that people respond more candidly and honestly when the confidentiality of their responses is ensured. Even if you used well-known, standardized tests (TAT or MMPI, for example), it is still a good idea to describe them in a few sentences. By describing them, you communicate to the reader that you truly understand the nature and purpose of the test you chose.

Incidentally, two valuable sources of background information on attitude scales and other social psychological measures are Marvin E. Shaw and Jack M. Wright's *Scales for the Measurement of Attitudes* (McGraw-Hill) and John P. Robinson, Phillip R. Shaver, and Lawrence S. Wrightsman's *Measures of Personality and Social Psychological Attitudes* (Academic Press). These reference books also may save you from having to "reinvent the wheel" because they contain reproductions of dozens of useful scales.

Results

In the next major section, describe your findings. You might plan to show the results in a table, as in Table 2 of John's report. Do not make your instructor guess what you are thinking; label your table fully and discuss the data in the narrative of this section so that it is clear what the numbers represent.

The results section should consist of a careful, detailed analysis that strikes a balance between being discursive and being falsely or needlessly precise.

- You are guilty of **false precision** when something inherently vague is presented in overly precise terms. Suppose you used one of the attitude scales in Shaw and Wright's book in your research, and suppose the research participants indicated their attitudinal responses by using a five-point scale of "strongly agree" to "strongly disagree." It would be falsely precise to report the means to a high number of decimal places, because your scale was not that sensitive to slight variations in attitudes.

- You are guilty of **needless precision** when (almost without thinking about it) you report something much more exactly than the circumstances require. For example, reporting the weight of mouse subjects to six decimal places might be within the bounds of your measuring instrument, but the situation does not call for such exactitude.

Note on page 6 of John's report that he gives the p-value of one of his results as .00000001. Is this a case of needless precision? In fact, it is a valuable piece of information if the reader wanted to use your data as part of a **meta-analysis** of all the results in this area. Instead of ending a research report with the usual clarion call for further research, a meta-analysis summarizes available studies in terms of such criteria as their significance levels and effect sizes. If you are interested in learning about meta-analysis, you might begin with Richard J. Light and David B. Pillemer's *Summing Up: The Science of Reviewing Research* (Harvard University Press). Notice also that John's paper gives the Z values to only two decimal places, which is perfectly correct (because he does not want to be guilty of needless precision).

Ask yourself the following questions as you structure your results section:

- What did I find?
- How can I say what I found in a careful, detailed way?
- Is what I am planning to say precise and to the point?
- Am I being overly or misleadingly exact?
- Will what I have said be clear to the reader?
- Have I left out anything of importance?

Discussion

In the discussion section you will use the facts you have gathered to form a cohesive unit. A review of the introductory section is often helpful. Think about how you will discuss your research findings in light of your original hypothesis. Did **serendipity** play a role in your study? The term comes from Serendip, once the name for Sri Lanka; it was claimed that the three princes of Serendip were always making discoveries by good luck. If serendipity has played a role in your study, detail the unexpected by-products and ideas.

Try to write "defensively"; that is, be your own devil's advocate. Look for shortcomings or critical inconsistencies and anticipate the reader's reaction to them.

Here are additional questions to consider as you begin to structure this section:

- What was the purpose of my study?
- How do my results relate to that purpose?
- Did I make any serendipitous findings of interest?
- How valid and generalizable are my findings?
- Are there larger implications in these findings?

You might wish to plan a separate conclusion section if you feel more comfortable with that format or have a lot to cover that you would like to separate from the main body of your discussion. However, it is quite proper to treat the final paragraph or two of your discussion section as the conclusion. In either case, your conclusions should be stated as clearly and concisely as possible.

If there were larger implications, this would be the place to spell them out. Are there implications for further research? If so, suggest them here. John implies the external validity question in the final paragraph of his discussion, in which he raises the need to replicate his findings in other naturalistic settings.

References

Once you have made plans for writing the body of the report, give some thought to your reference material again. You will need to include an alphabetized listing of all the sources of information from which you drew. To avoid retracing your steps in the library, **keep a running list** of the material that will appear in this section as you progress through the early preparation of the report. If you are using a word processor, then add each reference to the back of the report as you cite it in your narrative. If you are using the index-card method, then make a separate card for each reference that you actually use in your report; it will be a simple matter later to alphabetize the cards and make sure that none have been omitted.

Appendix

The purpose of this final section is to display the raw materials and computations of your investigation. For example, if you used a lengthy questionnaire or test—which cannot be adequately presented in the limited space of the method section—then include it in the appendix. John's questionnaire was so brief and straightforward that he was able to present it fully in a couple of sentences, but he includes his statistical calculations in the appendix.

Your instructor may not require an appendix or may stipulate a different list of items to be included. Keep all of your notes and data until the instructor returns your report and you receive a grade in the course, just in case your instructor has questions about your work.

Organizing Your Thoughts

In the preceding chapter we described how to make an outline for the term paper; the research report does not require an outline because its formal structure already provides a skeleton waiting to be fleshed out. Nevertheless, most researchers find it absolutely essential to organize their thoughts about each section before writing the first draft. There are two ways to do this:

- If you like to work with a detailed sentence outline, then read Chapter 3 for guidelines.

- Or you can make notes on separate index cards for each major point (e.g., rationale of the study, derivation of each hypothesis, and each background study) and draw on these notes to write your first draft. If you are using a word processor, then you can simply make a file of such notes.

If you still are having a hard time getting going, here are two more tips:

- Imagine you are sitting across a table from a friend; tell your "friend" what you found.

- Take a pocket tape recorder for a walk; tell it what you found in your research.

No matter what approach you favor, make sure that your notes or files are accurate and complete. If you are summarizing someone else's study, you must note the full citation. If you are quoting someone, include the statement in quotation marks and make sure that you have copied it exactly.

5

Writing and Revising

Writing a first draft is a little like taking the first dip in chilly ocean waters on a hot day. It may be uncomfortable at the outset but feels better once you get used to it. In this chapter we provide some pointers to buoy you up as you begin writing. We also shall provide tips to help you revise your work.

Focusing on the Objective

At this stage of your work, you should have an ordered set of notes and an outline, in the case of the term paper, or a given structure if your project is a research report. The material you have assembled can be thought of as the bare bones of the paper. Sentences and paragraphs will be combined now to fill out the skeleton.

To begin the first draft, write down somewhere the purpose or goal you have in mind. Make this **self-motivator statement** succinct so that you have a focus for your thoughts as you begin to set them down on paper or enter them on the screen and memory of a word processor.

If we refer to the two sample papers, we can imagine the following self-motivators:

From Maria

I'm going to write an expository term paper that will describe two general modes of treatment for anorexia nervosa.

From John

> My relational research report will focus on whether people are more likely to pass on rumors they feel are true as opposed to rumors they don't feel are true.

This trick of using a self-motivator statement can help to keep your mind focused and make the task of writing seem less formidable. The self-motivator is a good way simply to get you going, and you will be less apt to go off on a tangent if you remind yourself exactly where you want your paper to go.

Settling Down to Write

A good opening sentence is crucial to a good paper. A paradoxical statement, a definition, an anecdote, or a colorful simile or metaphor that compares or contrasts—all of these are devices that a writer can use to shape the paper's opening sentence. Not only will it draw the reader into the paper but also it will serve to provide momentum for you, the writer, as words and ideas begin to flow.

- John, for instance, starts with a fact: "Rumor is traditionally defined as a proposition for belief that is unverified and in general circulation." By tying this information to an illustrative reference ("e.g., Allport & Postman, 1947"), he also informs the reader that work on this topic reaches back many years and that he is aware of that early work.

- Maria, on the other hand, begins her paper by pointing up a paradox: "In a society in which food is plentiful and indeed a topic of almost obsessive interest and concern, it seems paradoxical that an eating disorder can be so prevalent." The statement arrests the reader's attention and may make the project stand out in the group of papers the instructor is reading.

Should you find yourself having trouble beginning the introductory paragraph, try the trick of not starting at the opening of your paper. Start writing whatever section you feel will be easiest, and then tackle the rest as your ideas begin to flow. When faced with the blank page or blank computer screen and flashing cursor, some students escape by taking a nap or watching MTV. Recognize these counterproductive moves for what they are, and use them instead as rewards after you have done your work.

The following are general pointers to ensure that your writing will go as smoothly as possible:

- While writing, try to work in a quiet, well-lighted place in two-hour stretches. Go for a walk by yourself to collect your thoughts and to think of a sentence to get you going again.

- If you are typing your first draft, double- or triple-space it so you will have room for legible revisions. If you are writing on a note pad, skip a line for each line you write down. If you are using a word processor, modify the system format to double-space your printout.

- Be sure to number the pages you write. If you are using a word processor, modify the system format so the page numbers will automatically appear as they do in Maria's and John's papers.

- When you take a break, try to stop at a point that is midway through an idea or a paragraph. In this way you can resume work where you left off and avoid feeling stuck or having to start cold. If you are using a word processor, type in a line of X's to show yourself where you left off.

- Try to pace your work with time to spare so that you can complete the first draft and let it rest for 24 hours. When you return to the completed first draft after a break, your critical powers will be enhanced and you will have a fresh approach to shaping the final draft.

Plagiarism

Before you actually start writing, let us return to the subject of **plagiarism,** which was mentioned briefly in Chapter 2. The term comes from a Latin word meaning "kidnapper," and in current literary usage it refers to kidnapping another person's ideas or work and passing them off as your own. A recent book on this subject is Thomas Mallon's *Stolen Words: Forays into the Origins and Ravages of Plagiarism* (Penguin, 1991). In one fascinating case described by Mallon, CBS television and the creators of *Falcon Crest* were sued for plagiarism by the author of a novel about the California wine country. It is crucial that you understand what constitutes plagiarism and the consequences that result for those who commit it. Plagiarism in student writing is often accidental, but it is important to avoid "kidnapping" someone else's work even if you do so unintentionally. For students, the penalties for plagiarism in a class assignment can be severe.

This does not mean that you cannot use other people's ideas or work in your writing. What it does mean, however, is that you must give the author of that material full credit for originality and not misrepresent (intentionally or accidentally) that material as your own original work. To illustrate, imagine that a student submitted a term paper containing the following paragraph:

> Deceit and violence are two forms of deliberate assault on human beings. Both can coerce people into acting against their will. Most harm that can happen to people through violence can also happen to them through deceit. However, deceit controls more subtly, because it works on belief as well as action. Even Othello, whom few would have dared to try to subdue by force, could be brought to destroy himself and Desdemona through falsehood.

Sounds like an "A" paper? Yes, but the student would be failed, at the very least. The reason for the student's "F" is plagiarism. The student "lifted" a passage out of Sissela Bok's *Lying: Moral Choice in Public and Private Life* (Pantheon, 1978) without indicating that the work was Bok's. On page 18 of her book, Bok states as follows:

> Deceit and violence—these are the two forms of deliberate assault on human beings. Both can coerce people into acting against their will. Most harm that can befall victims through violence can come to them also through deceit. But deceit controls more subtly, for it works on belief as well as action. Even Othello, whom few would have dared to try to subdue by force, could be brought to destroy himself and Desdemona through falsehood.

How might the student have used Bok's work without falling into plagiarism? The answer is simply to put quotes around the material you want to copy verbatim—and then give a complete citation. Even if you wanted simply to paraphrase the work, you still are responsible for giving full credit to the original author. A reasonable paraphrase might appear as follows:

> Bok (1978) makes the case that deceit and violence "both can coerce people into acting against their will" (p. 18). Deceit, she notes, controls more subtly, because it affects belief. Using a literary analogy, she observes: "Even Othello, whom few would

have dared to try to subdue by force, could be brought to destroy himself and Desdemona through falsehood" (p. 18).

Lazy Writing

Some lazy students, upon hearing that quotations and citations are not construed by definition as plagiarism, sometimes submit papers consisting almost entirely of quoted material. Unless you feel that it is absolutely essential, avoid quoting long passages throughout a paper. It may be necessary to quote or paraphrase some material (with a citation, of course), but your written work is expected to result from your own individual effort.

That is, your paper should reflect *your* thoughts on a particular topic after you have researched and synthesized material from the sources you feel are pertinent. The penalty for lazy writing is not as severe as that for plagiarism, although it often still is a reduced grade. Avoid both problems—plagiarism and lazy writing. As noted earlier, it is a good idea to keep your note cards, outlines, and rough drafts, because some instructors will ask students for such material if a question arises about the originality of their work.

And finally, many students use terms that they do not understand, especially when dealing with technical material—anatomical or statistical terms, for example. Although this is not considered plagiarism, it also constitutes lazy writing. Always try to make your point in your own words. If someone else has said it much better than you ever can hope to say it, quote (and cite) or paraphrase (and cite) the other source. On the other hand, if you really cannot say it in your own words, then you do not understand it well enough to write about it.

Tone

As you write, there are certain style points to keep in mind. The **tone** of your paper refers to the way in which it approaches the reader. Your writing should not be dull; presumably you are writing on a topic that you find fascinating, inasmuch as you chose it.

Some hints on how to create the right tone follow:

• Strive for an explicit, straightforward, interesting but not emotional way of expressing your thoughts, findings, and conclusions.

- Avoid having your term paper or research report read like a letter to a favorite aunt ("Here's what Jones and Smith say . . ." or "So I told the research participants . . .").

- Do not try to duplicate a journalist's slick "newspeak" style, familiar in the glib spoken reports on network TV and in popular magazines.

- It is all right to use the first person ("I shall discuss . . ." or "My conclusion is that . . ."). However, do not refer to yourself as *we*, unless you have a split personality and both of you collaborated on the paper ("We observed that . . ." or "In this paper we will explore . . .").

- Strive for an objective, direct tone that keeps your reader subordinate to the material you are presenting. Do not write: "The reader will note that the results were . . ." Instead write: "The results were . . ."

- A famous writing manual is that by William Strunk, Jr. and E. B. White, *The Elements of Style* (Macmillan). One of Professor Strunk's admonitions is: "Omit needless words. Omit needless words. Omit needless words."

Study the following excerpts lifted from the sample papers to see how the tone used by the student can color the impact of the paper. John states his hypothesis in response to a question he poses that piques our interest; he uses the impersonal pronoun *one* to make a general statement and in this way avoids the awkward *he/she* or *s/he* contraction that inexperienced writers fall into.

From John's research report

Why is it that some rumors are transmitted with greater alacrity than others during stressful situations? In this study it was hypothesized that the more confidence one has in the truth of a rumor, the more likely one is to transmit the rumor.

Maria also describes the problem she chose to study in a tone that is compelling but not melodramatic or slick, and she uses the first person *I* to draw the reader into her paper.

From Maria's term paper

Often in victims of the disorder a distorted body image is apparent. They starve themselves to achieve dramatic weight loss; yet in spite of their emaciated appearance they perceive themselves to be layered in fat, a condition they are determined to control. In this paper I shall discuss two major treatments of anorexia nervosa.

Gender

The question of **word gender** has become a matter of some sensitivity among writers, especially those working in psychology. In the interests of equality of the sexes as well as in writing precision, the student writer should avoid the archaic use of the masculine gender in nouns and pronouns when referring to both men and women—for example, "man and his world" when you mean "people and their world."

Beware of masculine nouns and pronouns that can give a sex bias to your writing that you do not intend. There are two simple rules.

- Use plural pronouns when you are referring to both genders; for instance, "They did . . ." instead of "He did . . ." or " . . . to them" instead of " . . . to him."

- Use masculine and feminine pronouns if the situation calls for them. For example, if the study you are discussing used only male research participants, then the masculine pronoun *he* is accurate; the contraction *he/she* or *s/he* would mislead the reader into thinking that the research participants included both sexes.

Voice

The verb forms you use in your writing can speak with one of two voices—active or passive. You write in the **active voice** when you represent the subject of your sentence as performing the action expressed by your verb ("The research participants responded by . . ."). You write in the **passive voice** when the subject of your sentence undergoes the action expressed by your verb ("The response made by the research participants was . . .").

If you try to rely mainly on the active voice, then you will have a more vital, compelling style.

Active voice (good)

Dollard and Miller theorized that frustration leads to aggression.

Passive voice (not as good)

It was theorized by Dollard and Miller that frustration leads to aggression.

However, the passive voice sometimes is useful to avoid the gender traps of singular masculine pronouns when you actually mean to refer to both sexes. For example:

Active (gender trap)

If the subject reacted in this way, it was taken to be a clear indication of his political attitude.

Passive (no gender trap)

A particular political attitude was clearly indicated by the subject's reaction.

Verb Tense

The **verb tense** you use in your paper can get into a tangle unless you observe the following basic rules:

- Use the **past tense** to report studies that were done in the past ("Jones and Smith found . . ."). If you are writing a research report, then both method and results sections call for the past tense because your study already has been accomplished ("In this study, rumors *were collected* . . ." and "In these 55 questionnaires there *were* . . .").
- Use the **present tense** to define terms ("Thus anorexia nervosa, in clinical parlance, *refers* to . . ." and "Rumor *is* traditionally defined as . . ."). The present tense also is used frequently to state a general hypothesis or to make a general claim ("A current rumor theory *suggests* that the strength of a rumor *is* determined by . . .").

- The **future tense** can be saved for the section of your paper in which you discuss implications for further investigation ("Future research *will be* necessary . . ."), but it is not essential to use the future tense. For instance, John uses the present tense effectively ("Further investigation *is* warranted . . .").

Agreement of Subject and Verb

Make sure each sentence expresses a complete thought and has a **subject** (in general terms, something that performs the action) and a **verb** (an action to perform or a state of being).

Subject and verb agree

Participants [**subject**] were [**verb**] faculty members.

Because the subject is plural (*participants*), the verb form used (*were*) also is plural. This means the verb and subject agree, which is a basic rule of grammar.

In most sentence forms, achieving this agreement is a simple matter. But trouble can sometimes arise:

- When you use **collective nouns** (those that name a group), they can be either singular or plural—for example, committee, team, faculty. When you think of the group as a single unit, use a singular verb ("The administration *is* ready to settle."). Plurals are called for when you want to refer to the components of a group ("The faculty *were* divided on the strike issue . . .").
- Trouble can pop up when words come between subject and verb: "Therapy [**singular subject**], in combination with behavioral organic methods of weight gain, exemplifies [**singular verb form**] this approach." It would be incorrect to write: "Therapy, in combination with behavioral organic methods of weight gain, *exemplify* [**plural verb form**] this approach."
- Use a **singular verb form** after the following: *each, either, everyone, someone, neither, nobody.* Here is a correct usage: "When everyone is ready, the experiment will begin."

Common Usage Errors

Instructors see frequent usage errors in student papers. The inside front cover of this manual lists pairs of words that are both pronounced similarly (**homonyms**) and often confused with one another, such as *accept* (to receive) and *except* (other than).

Another pair of confusing homonyms is *affect* and *effect*. *Affect*, a verb, means "to influence" (e.g., frustration can *affect* how a person behaves); as a noun, effect means an "outcome" (e.g., aggression is often an *effect* of frustration). *Affect* has a special meaning when used as a noun in psychology; it is a synonym for "emotion" (e.g., the subjects showed positive *affect*).

Another potential source of problems is the correct use of the singular and plural of some familiar terms, for instance:

Singular	*Plural*
analysis	analyses
anomaly	anomalies
appendix	appendixes or appendices (both are correct)
criterion	criteria
datum	data
hypothesis	hypotheses
phenomenon	phenomena
stimulus	stimuli

Other common usage errors in psychology papers include the following:

- One is the confusion of *phenomena* (**plural term**) with *phenomenon* (**singular term**). It would be incorrect to write "This [**singular pronoun**] phenomena [**plural subject**] is [**singular verb**] of interest. . . ." The correct form is either "This phenomenon is . . ." or "These phenomena are . . ."

- Another common error results from the confusion of *data* (**plural term**) with *datum* (**singular term**). It would be incorrect to write "The data [**plural subject**] indicates [**singular verb**] . . ." The correct form is either "The data indicate . . ." or "The datum indicates . . ."

- Another problem frequently occurs with the words *between* and *among*. Use *between* when you are referring to two items only; use *among* when there are more than two items. It would be incorrect to write "between the three of them." It would be correct to say "The differences *between* the experimental and control conditions were . . ." or "Age and educational level *among* the four groups of respondents indicate . . ."

- There is, however, one anachronism that you can do nothing about correcting. In the analysis of variance, conventional usage is to speak of the "between sum of squares," and the "between mean square," even if the number of conditions being compared is more than two!

Other common problems concern the use of some **prefixes** in psychological terms:

- The prefix *inter-* means "between" (interpersonal, or between persons); the prefix *intra-* means "within" (intrapersonal, within the person).

- The prefix *intro-* means "inward" or "within"; the prefix *extra-* means "outside" or "beyond." The psychological term *introverted* thus refers to an "inner-directed personality"; the term *extraverted* indicates an "outer-directed personality."

- The prefix *hyper-* means "too much"; the prefix *hypo-* means "too little." Hence, the term *hypothyroidism* refers to a deficiency of thyroid hormone, while *hyperthyroidism* denotes an excess of thyroid hormone. A *hyperactive* child is one who is excessively active.

Punctuation

Correct use of the various punctuation marks will ensure that your writing is clear. A **period** ends a declarative sentence. It also follows an abbreviation, as in the following common abbreviations of Latin words:

cf.	from *confer* ("compare")
e.g.	from *exempli gratia* ("for example")
et al.	from *et alia* ("and others")
et seq.	from *et sequens* ("and following")
ibid.	from *ibidem* ("in the same place")
i.e.	from *id est* ("that is")
op. cit.	from *opere citato* ("in the work cited")
viz.	from *videlicet* ("namely")

If you continually wrote "eg." or "et. al." in your paper, you would be waving a red flag at your instructor. You would be telling the instructor, "I don't know the meaning of these terms!" The reason, of course, is that "e.g." is the abbreviation for two words not one, but "eg." announces that you believe it is the abbreviation of one word. Putting a period after "et" tells the instructor that you believe it is an abbreviation, which it is not.

On the subject of abbreviations, certain others that you may encounter in the library are the diminutives of English words:

anon.	from *anonymous*
ch.	from *chapter*
diagr.	from *diagram*
ed.	from *editor* or *edition*
fig.	from *figure*
ms.	from *manuscript*
p.	from *page*
pp.	from *pages*
rev.	from *revised*
vol.	from *volume*

The various uses of the **comma** include the following:

- Use commas to separate three or more items in a series ("Smith, Jones, and Brown" or "high, medium, and low scorers").
- Set off introductory phrases in a sentence with a comma ("In another experiment performed 10 years later, the same researchers found . . .").
- Use commas to set off thoughts or phrases that are not essential to qualify the meaning of the sentence ("This variable, which was incidental to the researchers' central hypothesis, was also examined . . .").
- Put a comma before connecting words (*and, but, or, nor, yet*) when they join independent clauses ("The subject lost weight, but he was still able to . . .").

The **semicolon** (;) is used to join independent clauses in a sentence when connecting words are omitted. A semicolon is called for when the thoughts in the two independent clauses are close and the writer wishes to emphasize this point or to contrast the two thoughts.

Semicolon for connecting thoughts

Anorexia nervosa is a disorder in which the victims literally starve themselves; despite this emaciated appearance, they consider themselves to be overweight.

In most instances, these long sentences can be divided into shorter ones, which will be clearer.

No semicolon

Anorexia nervosa is a disorder in which the victims literally starve themselves. Despite their emaciated appearance, they consider themselves to be overweight.

Use a **colon** (:) to indicate that a list will follow, to introduce a quotation, or to introduce an amplification. The colon tells the reader "note what follows."

Colon to indicate a list follows

Subjects were given the following items: (a) four calling birds, (b) three French hens, (c) two turtledoves . . .

Colon to indicate a quote follows

Subject B responded: "My feeling about this ridiculous situation is that we should leave."

Colon to introduce an amplication (e.g., John's title)

Confidence in Rumor and the Likelihood of Transmission:
A Correlational Study

Quotations

Double quotation marks (" ") are used to enclose direct quotations in the narrative of the paper, and **single quotation marks** (' ') indicate a quote within a quote.

Quotation marks

> Subject B responded: "My feeling about this ridiculous situation was summed up in a nutshell by Jim when he said, 'It's a tough job, but somebody has got to do it.' "

Here are more rules about punctuation when using quotations in your paper:

- If the appropriate punctuation is a comma or a period, it is included *within* the quotation marks.
- Colons and semicolons always come *after* the closing quotation marks.
- When the quotation is more than four typed or handwritten lines, it is set off from the body of the prose by means of indented margins, and quotation marks are omitted.

Passage containing lengthy quotation and internal quotation

> What practical implications do Rosenthal and Jacobson (1968) draw from their research findings? They write:

> > As teacher-training institutions begin to teach the possibility that teachers' expectations of their pupils' performance may serve as self-fulfilling prophecies, there may be a new expectancy created. The new expectancy may be that children can learn more than had been believed possible, an expectation held by many educational theorists, though for quite different reasons. . . . The new expectancy, at the very least, will make it more difficult when they encounter the educationally disadvantaged for teachers to think, "Well, after all, what can you expect?" The man on the street may be permitted his opinions and prophecies of the unkempt children loitering in a dreary schoolyard. The teacher in the schoolroom may need to learn that those same prophecies within her may be fulfilled; she is no casual passer-by. Perhaps Pygmalion in the classroom is more her role. (pp. 181–182)

Notice that the quotation begins "As teacher-training institutions . . . " and ends " . . . in the classroom is more her role"; the page numbers on which this passage appears in Rosenthal and Jacobson's book are shown in parentheses at the end.

This passage was written before there were concerns about word gender, and the authors refer to "the man on the street" and to the teacher as "she." If you wished to make the point that the quoted passage ignored word gender, then you might insert the word *sic* (from the Latin "so thus," denoting that a word, phrase, etc., that appears strange or incorrect has been quoted verbatim) in brackets after the first pronoun. It then would look like this:

> schoolyard. The teacher in the schoolroom may need to learn that those same prophecies within her [sic] may be fulfilled

Revising

In the next chapter we consider the details of assembling and producing your final draft. Whether you are using a typewriter or a word processor, **revising** the first draft of your paper is best done after you have been able to leave the material entirely. When you approach your writing after having taken such a break (ideally, 24 hours or more), your critical powers will be sharper. Syntax errors, lapses in logic, and other problems will become evident, so that smoothing out these sections will be a relatively simple chore.

As you reread, consider the following "dos" and "don'ts":

- Be concise.
- Break up long paragraphs that contain a lot of disparate ideas into smaller, more coherent paragraphs.
- Be specific.
- Choose words for what they mean, not just for how they sound.
- Double-check punctuation.
- Don't use a long word when a short one will do.
- Don't be redundant ("most unique").
- Don't let spelling errors mar your writing.

If you are revising your first draft in longhand or with a typewriter, then equip yourself with scissors and glue the (retractable stick glue is the easiest to use). With these tools, rearranging paragraphs, condensing sentences, and adding or subtracting references can be less painful. The least painful recourse, however, is to use a word processor.

Using a Word Processor

If you are working with a **word processor** (i.e., a personal computer that uses a word-processing program), then you know that the steps involved in first drafts, revisions, and final drafts are telescoped. These stages lose their formal definition because the computer allows you, with the stroke of a key, to shift or change words, sentences, paragraphs, even entire sections as you compose. Notes, long quotations, references, tables, and even figures can be stored in the computer's hard drive or on a disk and retrieved as needed. Many word processors also allow you to use an automatic system to monitor your spelling of common English words. A word processor releases the writer from an enormous amount of drudgery, even though it is not a substitute for the hard work of organizing ideas, thinking them through, and expressing them clearly.

Always "back up" what you have written, and it is a good idea to do this every hour or so. You never know when the electricity will suddenly go out or someone will playfully or accidentally hit the erase key, sending your work into oblivion. Making a back-up means not only storing something inside the computer's memory (that is, if it's *your* PC) but also copying it onto a disk and making a printout (called a **hard copy**). Making a hard copy will allow you to inspect and modify the final layout to make sure it looks like Maria's or John's paper. It allows you to polish your writing in a format that is tangible. Sometimes spelling errors that are less evident on-screen jump out as your eye traverses a printed page.

Do not expect a perfect result on the first draft or even the second draft. Putting thoughts down on paper and revising them is a way of showing ourselves that we have made progress. It gives us something concrete to work on as we proceed to the final draft.

6

Layout and Production

Whether you use a word processor or a typewriter, you need to be concerned with the layout of your research report or term paper. This chapter, which uses Maria's and John's papers as illustrative models, will provide you with tips and general guidelines to develop a finished product.

The First Impression

Study the sample passage at the top of Exhibit 9. If you were the instructor and a student submitted a paper to you that began with this paragraph, what would your first impression be? How many problems did you notice? Did you catch the following problems?

- **typographical error:** Pygmaliom
- **spelling mistake:** Jacobsen [twice]
- **usage error:** phenomena
- **omission:** statistically significant
- **spelling mistake:** surpased
- **usage error:** &
- **typographical error:** inthe
- **spelling mistake:** intellectule

With a little time and effort the paragraph could have been cleaned up to enhance the student's finished product. Compare the messy paragraph with the carefully edited and cleanly prepared

Exhibit 9   First Impressions Count!

In Pygmalio*n* in the Classroom, Rosenthal and Jacobsen (1968) conclude that the phenomena of the self-fulfilling prophecy is as viable in the classroom as Rosenthal and his coworkers previously showed it to be in the scientist's laboratory. Students whose names were *statistically significant* randomly selected and represented to be "bloomers" showed IQ gains that surpased those of students not so labeled for their teachers. It was the label, Rosenthal & Jacobsen assert, which created false positive expectations in the teachers' minds and, in turn, resulted in this difference in intellectule performance.

In Pygmalion in the Classroom, Rosenthal and Jacobson (1968) conclude that the phenomenon of the self-fulfilling prophecy is as viable in the classroom as Rosenthal and his coworkers previously showed it to be in the scientist's laboratory. Students whose names were randomly selected and represented to be "bloomers" showed statistically significant IQ gains that surpassed those of students not so labeled for their teachers. It was the label, Rosenthal and Jacobson assert, which created false positive expectations in the teachers' minds and, in turn, resulted in this difference in intellectual performance.

paragraph below it to see what a difference a first impression can make. In the previous chapter we advised you to make backup copies if you were working with a word processor. Another reason for having a backup hard copy (i.e., a printout) is to allow you to evaluate and polish the layout of the anticipated finished product. The hard copy can look deceptively clean, so do not be captivated by the finished look of the printed page. Check it carefully against the sample papers for layout, and also check to make sure it is not flawed by errors of omission or lapses in logic.

General Pointers

We assume (as your instructor does) that you will correct spelling mistakes, usage errors, and omissions before you submit your paper. What follows are general pointers as you set about typing or processing that final draft:

- If you are typing the paper, treat yourself to a new typewriter ribbon. If you are using a word processor, find out if there is a laser printer you can use. If you are using an impact printer, make sure it has a fresh ribbon. It will be frustrating for the instructor to have to read a paper with script so light or blurry that it taxes the eyes.

- If you are typing the paper, use $8\frac{1}{2}$ x 11-inch white paper, preferably bond. Never use onionskin paper, because it tears easily and does not take corrections well. Do not use commercial "erasable" paper, because it smears readily.

- Use double line spacing and print or type on only one side of the paper, numbering pages in the upper-right corner as the sample papers illustrate.

- Make an extra copy of the finished paper, whether you are typing it or using a word processor. The original is for your instructor, and the duplicate copy will ensure that there is an exact spare copy available in case of an unforeseen problem.

- If you are using a word processor and do not have access to a laser or a daisy-wheel printer, use the strikeover (or letter-quality) mode rather than the first-draft mode to print your final copy.

- If you are using a word processor, let the right margin remain ragged. That is, do not use a justified right margin: It creates a block effect with sometimes odd spacing within lines. It is better to stick with a ragged right margin.

- Use generous margins to leave space for the instructor to make comments. When typing, set your pica typewriter at 55 characters per line; for an elite, use 66 per line.

We turn now to other specifics of layout and processing (or typing) that will help to give your finished product an inviting look.

Title Page Format

Glance at the title pages of Maria's and John's papers. Note that the title of the term paper or research report summarizes the main idea of the project and is centered on the page. A good title is succinct and yet adequately descriptive so that it gives the reader the gist of the work at a glance. Most likely, you already will have arrived at a working title when you narrowed your topic. That title can now be changed or made more specific if you feel it is no longer accurate or completely descriptive of the finished project.

The other information shown on the title page of Maria's and John's papers is:

- the student's name,
- the course or sequence for which the paper was written, and
- the date the paper was turned in.

It is optional to show the instructor's name (if submitted for a course) or the advisor's name (if submitted to fulfill some other requirement) on the cover page. However, if it is a senior honors thesis, you should include an acknowledgment page (after the title page) on which you thank your advisor and any others who extended a helping hand as you worked on your project.

Headings

It is customary to break up the text of a manuscript with headings. You can derive these from the outline of your term paper or, in the case of the research report, use the specific headings inherent in the structure of the report (Introduction, Method, and so on). Note how Maria's headings and subheadings lend symmetry to her paper, showing its progressive development in concise phrases.

Background

<u>Nature of the Problem</u>

<u>Treatment Approaches</u>

The Weight Gain Approach

<u>Behavioral Examples</u>

<u>Organic Examples</u>

The Weight Gain-Plus-Therapy Approach

Overview and Examples

Family Therapy

Conclusions

Maria's term paper uses two formats of headings: center and flush left. The **center heading** is used to separate the manuscript into major sections and is written in uppercase and lowercase letters and not underlined. To subdivide the major sections, she uses **sub-headings** placed at the left margin (flush left), underlined, and in uppercase and lowercase. If she wished to use another level of sub-headings, they would be indented, underlined, and followed by a period, with the body of the text immediately following the heading, for example:

Nature of the Problem
  Definition. Anorexia nervosa refers to . . .

Underlining

As this example shows, **underlining** can be used to distinguish levels of headings. Conventional usage also calls for the titles of books mentioned in the body of the text to be underlined ("In Pygmalion in the Classroom, Rosenthal and Jacobson . . . "). Underlining also is used in several other ways:

- Letters used as statistical symbols are underlined: F, N, n, P, p, t, Z, and so forth. However, Greek letters used as symbols are not underlined, for example, χ^2, Σ, σ.

- In reference lists, volume numbers of journal articles and titles of books and journals are underlined.

- Words that you wish to emphasize are underlined, but this should be done sparingly ("Effective teaching, the authors assert, will come only from the teachers' firm belief that their pupils can perform. . . . ").

Citations in Text

Several simple conventions are recommended by the APA Manual when citing an author's work in the narrative of a paper. The purpose of a citation is to make it easy for the reader to identify the source of a quotation or idea and then to locate the particular reference in the list at the end of the paper.

• The author–date method is the general format recommended. The surname of the author and the year of publication are inserted in the narrative text at the appropriate point.

• Do not list any publication in your reference list that you do not cite.

• Do not cite any reference without placing it in the reference list.

• If you want to cite a source that you did not read, use the following format: "Orne (1962), as cited by Sigall, Aronson, and Van Hoose (1970), postulated that . . . " But do this only if the original source is truly unavailable to you; otherwise examine and cite the original source yourself.

In general, there are two categories of citations in student research reports and term papers; you will find examples of each in Maria's and John's papers. One category consists of citations that appear as part of the narrative; the other category consists of citations inserted in alphabetical order (and then by year if the same author is cited twice) entirely in parentheses within the narrative.

Citation appearing as part of narrative

Jaeger, Anthony, and Rosnow (1980) planted a rumor among college students.

Citation entirely in parentheses

Lithium carbonate has been found to increase the anorectic's intake of fatty foods and thus produce weight gain (Gross, Evert, Goldberg, Faden, Nee, & Kaye, 1980).

These two examples also illustrate some of the conventions of author–date citations. First, the surnames of all authors are listed (even though in the latter instance this called for six names to be mentioned). It is customary to list all surnames the first time the citation is given, and in subsequent citations to mention only the surname of the first author followed by "et al." and the date, for example:

Subsequent citation as part of narrative

This finding is consistent with that of Jaeger et al. (1980) as previously discussed.

Subsequent citation entirely in parentheses

As mentioned, lithium carbonate was also found to be effective in producing weight gain (Gross et al., 1980).

Notice that the word *and* is spelled out in the narrative citation but that an ampersand (&) is used in the parenthetical citation. This is also conventional usage as recommended by the APA Manual. Other specific rules that cover most simple cases are:

- If you are citing a series of works, the proper sequence is by alphabetical order of the surname of the first author and then by the chronological order (Bender, 1990; Fisher, 1945, 1960; Kern, 1960, 1961; Mithalal, 1963, 1964).
- Two works published by the same author in the same year are designated as a, b, c, and so on (1980a, 1980b, 1980c). Alphabetical order of the works' titles determines their sequence.
- Work accepted for publication but not yet printed is designated as "in press" (Bender, in press); in a list of citations, the rule is to place this work last (Murphy, 1980, 1981, in press).

What should you do if you run into a problem that these rules do not address? If your instructor is a stickler for the APA style of handling citations, then ask the instructor or look in the APA Manual. We are not sticklers and only recommend that you keep one general idea in mind as you work within these specific guidelines: **If you run into a problem, use common sense.** Ask yourself whether you could find the one reference referred to based on the citation you provided. In other words, put yourself in your reader's shoes. For the reader, the citations are like the legend on a map, except that these legends are the key to the reference sources that you list at the end of your paper.

Tables and Figures

As with the title page (and the abstract of the research report), present each table and figure on a separate sheet of paper. Often, when students include tables in their research reports, the instructor finds that they merely are presenting their raw data in a neat format. Save your raw data for the appendix of your report (if this is required), and keep in mind that statistical tables in research reports are **summaries** of raw data (see Table 2 of John's report) and other results.

As John's report illustrates, a table is placed on a separate page and inserted just after the one on which it is first introduced in the narrative. To make it easy for the reader to locate, John states: "Examples of these two kinds of rumors are listed in Table 1 (see page 7)." Notice on page 7 of John's paper that the title is shown above the table, is underlined, and all information in the table is double-spaced.

It is also possible to use a **figure,** which in APA parlance refers to any type of exhibit or illustration other than a table. An easy way to differentiate between tables and figures is to think of tables in journal articles as typeset but figures as photographed from artwork. Had John used a figure to illustrate the information in his Table 2, it might have looked like this:

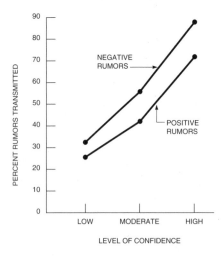

Figure 1. Transmission rate as a function of low, moderate, and high confidence in truth of negative and positive rumors.

Observe that the caption goes below the figure, and that it uses both uppercase and lowercase letters. If you are working with a word processor that has a graphics program, then you can compose the figure using the computer. Two entertaining books on the development of such graphics are Edward R. Tufte's *The Visual Display of Quantitative Information* and *Envisioning Information* (both published by Graphics Press). As Tufte points out, sometimes elaborate figures can introduce distortions, thus distracting from a clear, concise summary of the data.

However you choose to display your findings in the research report, the title or caption must be clearly and precisely stated. If you need to add some clarifying or explanatory note to your table, it is customary to place this information below the table.

Table note

Note. The possible range of scores was from 1 (strong disagreement) to 5 (strong agreement), with 3 indicating no opinion.

If you want to make specific notes, use superscript lowercase letters (^{a}, ^{b}, ^{c}) or asterisks (*, **, ***).

Superscript notation

$^a\underline{n} = 50$ $^b\underline{n} = 62$

Asterisk notation

$^*\underline{p} < .05$ $^{**}\underline{p} < .01$ $^{***}\underline{p} < .005$

In the latter case, however, we prefer to see exact *p*-values reported because of their utility in meta-analyses (discussed in Chapter 4).

The following guidelines will prove helpful if you are preparing a figure:

- The figure should be neat, clearly presented, and precisely labeled to augment your discussion.
- The figure should be large enough to read easily.
- When graphing the relationship between an independent variable and a dependent variable (or between a predictor variable and a criterion variable), it is customary to put the independent

(or predictor) variable on the horizontal axis and the dependent (or criterion) variable on the vertical axis.

- There are exceptions to the above convention, such as "stem-and-leaf" plots, developed by John W. Tukey and described in his book *Exploratory Data Analysis* (Addison-Wesley, 1977) as well as in many research-methods and statistics texts in psychology.
- The units should progress from small to large.
- The data should be precisely plotted. If you are drawing the figure by hand, use graph paper to help you keep the rows and columns evenly spaced.

Reference List

The reference list starts on a new page. The order of references is arranged alphabetically by the surname of the author(s) and then by the date of publication. The standard style is to:

- Invert all authors' names (i.e., last name, first name, middle initial). List authors' names in the exact order they appear on the title page of the publication. Use commas to separate authors and an ampersand (&) before the last author.
- Give the year the work was copyrighted (the year and month for magazine articles and the year, month, and day for newspaper articles).
- For book titles, capitalize only the first word of the title and of the subtitle (if any) as well as any proper names.
- For journal titles, capitalize the first word of the title and of the subtitle (if any), and all other words except coordinating conjunctions (*and, or*), articles (*a, an, the*), and prepositions (*in, of, for*).
- Give the issue number of the journal if an article cited is paginated by issue.
- Underline the volume number of a journal article and the title of a book or the name of a journal.
- Give the city of a book's publisher.
- If the city is not well known or might be confused with another location (for instance, Cambridge, Massachusetts, and Cam-

bridge, England), give the state (or country). When in doubt about whether to list the state, list it. Use the postal abbreviation; for instance, MA for Massachusetts.

Using these pointers, the examples in Maria's and John's papers, and the following examples as general guidelines, you should encounter no problems. If you do run into one, however, the rule of thumb is to be clear, consistent, and complete in listing your source material.

Authored book

Kimmel, A. J. (1988). Ethics and values in applied social research. Beverly Hills, CA: Sage.

Lana, R. E. (1969). Assumptions of social psychology. New York: Appleton-Century-Crofts.

Levin, J., & Arluke, A. (1987). Gossip: The inside scoop. New York: Plenum.

Work in press

Fine, G. A. (in press). The city as a folklore generator: Urban legends in the metropolis. Urban Resources.

Kapferer, J. (in press). Rumors: Uses, interpretations, and images. New Brunswick, NJ: Transaction Publishers.

Edited work

Gergen, K. J., & Gergen, M. (Eds.) (1984). Historical social psychology. Hillsdale, NJ: Erlbaum.

Morawski, J. G. (Ed.) (1988). The rise of experimentation in American psychology. New Haven, CT: Yale University Press.

Work republished at a later date

Demosthenes (1852). The Olynthiac and other public orations of Demosthenes. London: Henry G. Bohn. (Original work written 349 B.C.)

Journal article paginated by volume (three authors)

Arms, R. L., Russell, G. W., & Sandilands, M. L. (1979). Effects on the hostility of spectators' viewing aggressive sports. <u>Social Psychology Quarterly</u>, <u>42</u>, 275-279.

Article paginated by issue

Goldstein, J. H. (1978). In vivo veritas: Has humor research looked at humor? <u>Humor Research Newsletter</u>, <u>3</u>(1), 3-4.

Article in foreign language (title translated into English)

Foa, U. G. (1966). Le nombre huit dans la socialization de l'enfant [The number eight in the socialization of the infant]. <u>Bulletin du Centre d'Etudes et Recherches Psychologiques</u>, <u>15</u>, 39-47.

Jung, C. G. (1910). Ein Beitrag zur Psychologie des Gerüchtes [A contribution in the psychology of rumor]. <u>Zentralblatt fur Psychoanalyse</u>, <u>1</u>, 81-90.

Chapter in multivolume edited series

Kipnis, D. (1984). The use of power in organizations and interpersonal settings. In S. Oskamp (Ed.), <u>Applied social psychology</u> (Vol. 5, pp. 171-210). Beverly Hills, CA: Sage.

Koch, S. (1959). General introduction to the series. In S. Koch (Ed.), <u>Psychology: A study of a science</u> (Vol. 1, pp. 1–18). New York: McGraw-Hill.

Ross, L. (1977). The intuitive psychologist and his shortcomings: Distortions in the attribution process. In L. Berkowitz (Ed.), <u>Advances in experimental social psychology</u> (Vol. 10, pp. 174-214). Orlando, FL: Academic Press.

Magazine or newspaper article

Goldstein, J. H. (1982, August/September). A laugh a day: Can mirth keep disease at bay? <u>The Sciences</u>, pp. 21-25.

Rowan, R. (1979, August 13). Where did <u>that</u> rumor come from? <u>Fortune</u>, pp. 130-137.

Sexton, J. (1990, January 14). Rumors have effect on Rangers. <u>The New York Times</u>, Section 8, pp. 1, 4.

Doctoral dissertation abstract

Esposito, J. (1987). Subjective factors and rumor transmission: A field investigation of the influence of anxiety, importance, and belief on rumormongering (Doctoral dissertation, Temple University, 1986). <u>Dissertation Abstracts International</u>, <u>48</u>, 596B.

Technical report

Kipnis, D. M., & Kidder, L. H. (1977). <u>Practice performance and sex: Sex role appropriateness, success and failure as determinants of men's and women's task learning capabilities</u> (Report No. 1). Philadelphia, PA: University City Science Center.

Unpublished manuscript

Kimmel, A. J., & Keefer, R. (1989). <u>Psychological correlates of the acceptance and transmission of rumors about AIDS</u>. Unpublished manuscript, Fitchburg State College, Department of Behavioral Science, Fitchburg, MA.

Paper presented at a meeting

Lamberth, J. (1981, January). <u>Jury selection: A psychological approach</u>. Paper presented at the meeting of the American Trial Association, Moorestown, NJ.

Poster presented at a meeting

Walker, C. J., & Blaine, B. E. (1989, April). <u>The virulence of dread rumors: A field experiment</u>. Poster presented at the meeting of the Eastern Psychological Association, Boston, MA.

Proofing and Correcting

We now come to the final steps before you submit your paper: proofing and correcting. Read the finished manuscript more than once. Ask yourself the following questions:

- Are there omissions?
- Are there misspellings?
- Are the numbers correct?
- Are the hyphenations correct?
- Are all the references cited in the body of my paper in the references section, and vice versa? (Personal communications are only cited in the text, as Maria's page 7 illustrates.)

The first time you read your final draft, the appeal of the neat, clean copy can lead you to overlook errors. Put the paper aside for 24 hours, and then read it carefully again. If you find errors, then correct them before you submit the finished product. If they are small mistakes and you are typing the paper, then use correction fluid to cover them and make the required corrections. Do not just type over an incorrect letter or number. After typing a term paper or research report, however, it is permissible to insert an inadvertently omitted word or phrase *neatly* in the space above the line from which it was omitted. If there is a substantial omission or many such omissions, retype the entire page.

Give your paper a final look, checking to be sure all the pages are there and in order. If you adhered to the guidelines in this manual, you should have a sense of a job well done and feel confident that the paper will receive the serious attention that a clear, consistent, and attractive manuscript deserves.

Sample Term Paper

Major Treatments for Anorexia Nervosa:

Weight Gain Versus Weight Gain-Plus-Therapy

Maria Di Medio

Term Paper

Psych 156 Introduction to Abnormal Psychology

Cabrini College

(Date Submitted)

2

Abstract

Two major treatment approaches to anorexia nervosa are discussed. In one the focus was on weight gain, and in the other the focus was on weight gain as well as the patient's underlying psychological disorder(s). Several examples of each are described, and the conclusion drawn is that the combinatory approach is more effective. Background sources for this discussion include basic published findings and information obtained through correspondence with professionals.

Background

Nature of the Problem

  In a society in which food is plentiful and indeed a topic of
almost obsessive interest and concern, it seems paradoxical that an
eating disorder can be so prevalent. Anorexia nervosa is such a
disorder. The word anorexia derives from the Greek "want of
appetite," and in psychological and medical usage refers to "lack or
loss of appetite for food"; nervosa indicates a nervous condition.
Thus anorexia nervosa, in clinical parlance, refers to "a serious
nervous condition in which the patient loses his [her] appetite and
systematically takes but little food, so that he [she] becomes greatly
emaciated" (Dorland's Medical Dictionary, 1957, p. 94). Often in
victims of the disorder a distorted body image is apparent. They
starve themselves to achieve dramatic weight loss; yet in spite of
their emaciated appearance they perceive themselves to be layered
in fat, a condition they are determined to control.

Treatment Approaches

  In this paper I shall discuss two major treatments of anorexia
nervosa. One approach focuses on the treatment of the symptom of
significant weight loss. Operant conditioning, desensitization, the
administration of drugs and force feeding (hyperalimentation) are
elements of this treatment approach.

  The other approach treats the weight loss symptoms while
simultaneously focusing on the patient's psychological problems.
Variations of psychotherapy can be used to bolster the organic
procedures involved in effecting normal weight gain. The family's

4

relationship with the anorectic comes under scrutiny when family
therapy is the psychotherapeutic variation used to treat the
condition.

The Weight Gain Approach

Behavioral Examples

A 37-year-old anorectic weighed only 47 pounds when operant
conditioning treatment was begun (Bachrach, Erwin, & Mohr, 1965).
Initially she was deprived of any positive reinforcements (e.g.,
music, visitors). She then ate her meals in the presence of a
psychologist, medical student, or resident, who reinforced her
verbally when she made efforts to eat. Eventually, evidence of
weight gain became the criterion for reinforcement.

The patient's family continued reinforcing her efforts to eat,
and by the end of the program the patient weighed 88 pounds.
However, a follow-up study by Erwin (1977) 14 years later revealed
that the same patient's weight had dropped to 55 pounds, a result of
her not getting sufficient amounts of food. Despite her precarious
weight, the patient's social life improved as she became involved in
outside activities. Another study reports little difference in the
results of operant conditioning in hospital patients who received
behavior modification and those who did not (Eckert, Goldberg,
Halmi, Casper, & Davis, 1979).

Systematic desensitization is another behavioral approach in
the treatment of anorexia nervosa. It focuses on the anxiety
associated with eating and establishes a hierarchy for the specific
fear-eliciting stimuli (e.g., travel, disapproval, insecurity).

In one study, desensitization was used with a 23-year-old woman who had rapidly lost 20 pounds and displayed anxiety about eating (Lang, 1965). She often did not eat when she was in new surroundings or at odds with someone. During desensitization she was offered candy. Although she was desensitized, her problem could not be effectively remediated. However, it is questionable whether the subject had been properly diagnosed as having anorexia nervosa. Her refusal to eat may have been a reaction to stressful situations rather than an obsessive preoccupation with weight loss.

Behavioral treatment approaches are problematic at best. The weight gain achieved is rather short-lived, as the underlying psychological problems are left untreated (Bruch, 1979). Depriving anorectics of privileges has also been of questionable value as a treatment for the disorder (Bemis, 1978). An assessment of these modes of behavior therapy is difficult to achieve in that there have been few follow-up studies (Bemis, 1978). Also, small numbers of subjects have been used in the studies, and the effects of treatment have been clouded by the simultaneous administration of multiple medications to the patients involved (Eckert et al., 1979).

Organic Examples

Hyperalimentation (tube feeding) and drug therapy are two organic procedures that have been used in the treatment of anorexia nervosa. Lithium carbonate has been found to increase the patient's intake of fatty foods and thus produce weight gain (Gross, Evert, Goldberg, Faden, Nee, & Kay, 1980). It is not known how this drug directly affects weight, but it may have an effect on glucose

6

metabolism, which in turn affects one's desire to eat. Those treated with the drug did not deny their illness as much as those who did not receive the drug. Despite the weight gain associated with the use of the drug, the approach has been criticized because the patient's psychological well-being is not considered in this mode of treatment (Andersen, 1979; Bemis, 1978).

The Weight Gain-Plus-Therapy Approach

Overview and Examples

By far the more effective treatment for anorexia nervosa seems to be the combination of the establishment of a weight gain regimen accompanied or followed by psychotherapy for the patient and family members as well. One general view underlying the psychotherapeutic approach is that the victims are seen as perfectionists who strive to please the real or imagined standards of their families. Another view is that the behavior of patients is an attempt to manipulate their families in order to gain control over their own lives. Various combinations of weight gain treatments with therapy have been tried (Geller, 1975; Maloney & Farrell, 1980).

One study reported success with a behavioral method of individual therapy (Geller, 1975). A 22-year-old female not only gained weight but also felt more in control of her body after therapy. She was capable of expressing her feelings about eating more openly. Long-term results, however, were not reported. Hyperalimentation in combination with therapy has also proven effective in terms of weight gain, improved social behavior, enhanced concentration, and more facile expression of feelings (Maloney & Farrell, 1980).

Bruch (1979) recommends that weight gain precede therapy and that therapy begin when the patient weighs approximately 90-95 pounds. Another aspect of the therapy is to dispel maladaptive distortions about eating, thereby enhancing the patient's ability to see how the behavior adversely affects the body. Once the patient establishes a feeling of control over the body, it may be possible to generalize that feeling to other areas of life.

One integrated treatment approach (Lucas, Duncan, & Piens, 1976) consisted of (a) separating anorectics from their families, (b) establishing a weight gain approach by first having patients eat under supervision and then by themselves, (c) asking the patient to see a physiatrist to monitor weight goals and a therapist to treat distorted self-perception, and (d) counseling for the patient's family. This program was effective in improving anorectics' relationships with their families and friends and in alleviating the depression and listlessness the patients had experienced.

In another example (A. Andersen, personal communication, Nov. 10, 1980) of the integrated approach, the three-step treatment began with nutritional restitution (step 1). Then, when the patient was at 90-95 percent of ideal weight, individual, family, and group therapy (step 2) and restoration to the patient of eating responsibilities as well as other activities followed (step 3). Subsequently, the patient was checked to see whether he or she had readapted to the former environment without relapse. Approximately 50 percent improved with some symptoms remaining (e.g., preoccupation with food), while 25 percent remained very ill.

Family Therapy

Another treatment approach for the anorectic consists of directly involving the patient's family in helping the patient adjust. The patient's role in the family and family members' attitudes toward the disorder are considered. The patient usually undergoes behavior modification to change eating patterns. Then after the family has met with the professionals involved in the case, all (including the anorectic) have a luncheon session. It is structured so that the family's response to the patient's eating problem can be either strongly disapproving (badgering the patient about eating habits) or, at the other extreme, the family can "overlook" the problem (pretend it does not exist). Some families were reluctant to undertake this mode of treatment, perhaps concerned that long-buried family conflicts might surface. Out of 53 patients, 86 percent were effectively treated by family therapy (Minuchin, Rosman, & Baker, 1978).

                              Conclusions

In a comparison of two modes of treatment for anorexia nervosa, one focusing solely on weight gain, the other on weight gain-plus-therapy, there seems to be an indication that the latter approach is more effective. By addressing not only the patient's eating habits but also underlying personal conflicts and distorted perceptions, a more efficacious result can be predicted.

9

References

Andersen, A. (1979). Anorexia nervosa: Diagnosis and treatment. Weekly Psychiatry Update Series (Rep. 3). Princeton, NJ: Biomedia.

Bachrach, A., Erwin, W., & Mohr, J. (1965). The control of eating behavior in an anorectic by operant conditioning techniques. In L. P. Ullman & L. Krasner (Eds.), Case studies in behavior modification (pp. 153-163). New York: Holt, Rinehart & Winston.

Bemis, K. (1978). Current approaches to the etiology and treatment of anorexia nervosa. Psychological Bulletin, 85, 593-617.

Bruch, H. (1979). The golden cage: The enigma of anorexia nervosa. New York: Vintage.

Dorland's medical dictionary. (1957). Philadelphia, PA: Saunders.

Eckert, E., Goldberg, S., Halmi, K., Casper, R., & Davis, J. (1979). Behavior therapy in anorexia nervosa. British Journal of Psychiatry, 134, 55-59.

Erwin, W. (1977). A 16 yrs. follow up case of severe anorexia nervosa. Journal of Behavior and Experimental Psychiatry, 84, 157-160.

Geller, J. (1975). Treatment of anorexia nervosa by the integration of behavior therapy and psychotherapy. Psychotherapy and Psychosomatics, 26, 167-177.

Gross, H., Evert, M., Goldberg, S., Faden, V., Nee, L., & Kaye, W. (1980). A double blind controlled trial of lithium carbonate in primary anorexia nervosa. Unpublished manuscript, NIMH Clinical Center, Bethesda, MD.

Lang, P. (1965). Behavior therapy with a case of nervous anorexia. In L. Ullman & L. Krasner (Eds.), Case studies in behavior modification (pp. 217-221). New York: Holt, Rinehart & Winston.

Lucas, A., Duncan, J., & Piens, V. (1976). The treatment of anorexia nervosa. American Journal of Psychiatry, 133, 1034-1038.

10

Maloney, M., & Farrell, M. (1980). Treatment of severe weight loss in
anorexia nervosa with hyperalimentation and psychotherapy.
American Journal of Psychiatry, 137, 314-318.

Minuchin, S., Rosman, B., & Baker, L. (1978). Psychosomatic families:
Anorexia nervosa in context. Cambridge, MA: Harvard University
Press.

Sample Research Report

Confidence in Rumor and the Likelihood of Transmission:

A Correlational Study

John H. Yost

Research Report

Temple University Honors Sequence

Advisor: (Advisor's name)

(Date Submitted)

2

Abstract

Tense labor negotiations provided a setting of anxiety in which to study the transmission of rumors. Were individuals more likely to transmit rumors when they were confident of the truth of the rumor? This question was addressed to faculty members in the midst of labor negotiations between the union and university administration. Participants were asked to complete a questionnaire in which they reported any rumors that they had heard concerning the ongoing negotiations, to state whether or not they had transmitted the rumors, and to rate their confidence in the truth of the rumors. As hypothesized, there was a positive linear relationship between the amount of confidence and the likelihood of transmission of the rumor. The results are discussed in the context of recent rumor theory, and an idea for further investigation is suggested.

Introduction

Rumor is traditionally defined as a proposition for belief that is unverified and in general circulation (e.g., Allport & Postman, 1947). A current rumor theory (Rosnow, 1980) suggests that the strength of a rumor (and, therefore, the amount of rumor in circulation) is determined by a complex function of anxiety (an emotional factor) and uncertainty (a cognitive factor). These two conditions, when stimulated by ongoing events, are posited to be linearly related to rumor strength. Thus when a situation elicits little anxiety or uncertainty, the low levels of arousal generate no rumors. However, when a situation elicits higher levels of anxiety and uncertainty, there is a more urgent desire to reduce the emotional and cognitive unrest. That is, the greater the anxiety and uncertainty, the greater the need to alleviate discomfort.

Knapp (1944) observed that rumors thrive in periods of social stress. Current rumor theory is consistent with this observation, and different investigations of rumor concern periods of obvious discomfort, such as a catastrophe or a war (e.g., Allport & Lepkin, 1945; Knapp, 1944; Nkpa, 1975; Prasad, 1935), but none has actually collected data on the rate of rumor transmission. Data concerning the reasons individuals transmit certain rumors and not others would be valuable in helping to understand the phenomenon of rumormongering.

Why is it that some rumors are transmitted with greater alacrity than others during stressful situations? In this study it was hypothesized that the more confidence one has in the truth of a rumor, the more likely one is to transmit the rumor. This

4

hypothesis proceeds on the assumption that the credibility of the person passing the rumor is at stake when a rumor is transmitted. It should be to one's advantage to pass information that has a good chance of being true rather than information that is likely to prove false. Passing false rumors might jeopardize one's future credibility, while passing rumors that prove true would enhance one's future credibility.

There is already some experimental evidence that supports the idea of a relationship between confidence in rumor and rumor transmission. Jaeger, Anthony, and Rosnow (1980) planted a rumor among college students. In one condition the rumor was refuted by a confederate, and in another condition the rumor was not refuted. Subjects in the refutation groups reported lower initial belief in the rumor than subjects in the nonrefutation groups, and the rumor was circulated with lower frequency when refuted. The present study sought to determine whether this relationship found in an experimental setting with college students also held true in a field setting with a different population of subjects. The question addressed was whether there was a significant positive relationship between confidence in the truth of rumors and rumor transmission during a period of stressful labor negotiations.

Method

In this study, rumors were collected during a stressful period. A university community was divided over contract negotiations between the faculty union and the university administration. The faculty union had voted to strike if a contract agreement were not reached by a specific date. Publicly, the administration refused to negotiate on the faculty union's major demand. The university community was gripped with tension as the strike deadline approached. There was much speculation as to whether or not there would be a strike as well as what to do should a strike occur. The data in this study were collected in the week prior to the strike deadline, when tensions seemed relatively high. Only a last-minute settlement averted a strike, and most members of the university community were unclear about the situation until the final moments.

Questionnaires were placed in the interoffice mailboxes of 505 full-time faculty members from 28 different departments one morning, 10 days before the strike deadline that had been announced by the union. The instructions asked the recipients to list any rumors that they had heard over the past several days that pertained to the ongoing labor negotiations at the university. Rumor was defined as "any report, statement, or story that one may have heard or mentioned for which there is no immediate evidence available to verify its truth." After reporting each rumor the respondents were asked to indicate whether or not the rumor was transmitted and to rate their confidence in the truth of the rumor on a 0 to 10 scale. Zero represented "no confidence in the truth of the rumor" and 10 represented "strong confidence in the truth of the rumor." The anonymity of the respondents was assured, and they were asked to return the completed questionnaire through the interoffice mail within 7 days (3 days before the strike deadline). There were 55 questionnaires returned, for a response rate of 11 percent.

6

Results

    In these 55 questionnaires there were 134 responses purported to be "rumors" by the respondents. The 134 items were classified by two independent raters as positive rumors, negative rumors, or nonrumors. There were 20 items that were classified as nonrumors, leaving a total of 114 rumors. Rumors were classified as "positive" if the judges agreed that the outcome of the rumor would be beneficial to the respondent (i.e., beneficial to faculty members). Rumors were classified as "negative" if the judges agreed that the outcome of the rumor would be detrimental to the respondent (i.e., detrimental to faculty members). Examples of these two kinds of rumors are listed in Table 1 (see page 7). Of the 114 rumors reported, 22 were classified as positive and 92 as negative.

    Within both positive and negative categories the confidence ratings were collapsed to form three levels of confidence: low (ratings of 0 to 3), moderate (4 to 6), and high (7 to 10). The results are shown in Table 2 (see page 8) in terms of the percentage of positive and negative rumors reported as having been transmitted at each of the three levels of confidence. A linear trend analysis, employing the contrast procedure described by Rosenthal and Rosnow (1985), was used to analyze the data. As this table clearly shows, there was an increasing linear relationship between confidence in rumor and transmission rate.

    For negative rumors the Z of significance of the linear contrast was highly significant, with $Z = 5.67$, $p = .00000001$ one-tailed. The effect size was also impressive, with $r = .59$. For positive rumors the results were not as exciting statistically, but were impressive

7

Table 1

Sample Rumors

Positive rumors:

"Even if there were to be a strike, the faculty would not lose any pay."

"The administration is ready to settle."

Negative rumors:

"The administration wants a strike to break the union."

"All faculty benefits will be stopped if a strike occurs; also, salaries will be stopped."

8

Table 2

Rates of Transmission of Rumors

Confidence	Negative Rumors	Positive Rumors
High	86.1%	71.4%
Moderate	52.4%	42.9%
Low	31.4%	25.0%

nonetheless, with $Z = 2.00$, $p = .02$ one-tailed, $r = .43$. Although these results do not prove causality, they are consistent with the idea that individuals are more inclined to pass rumors that they believe than rumors that they do not believe.

Discussion

The findings are consistent with current rumor theory, which asserts that when a situation elicits high anxiety and uncertainty there is a more urgent desire to reduce the emotional and cognitive discomfort. This desire to alleviate discomfort will often result in rumor transmission where individuals try to make sense of a situation and to assess possible future outcomes. If someone has low confidence in the truth of a rumor, upon transmission this person's anxiety and uncertainty may not decrease. It may even increase because of the added stress of transmitting information that may be false and potentially damaging to one's credibility. Therefore, individuals may have a tendency not to pass a rumor when they do not have much confidence in its veracity. On the other hand, the more confidence people have in the truth of a rumor, the more effective will be the alleviation of discomfort as they transmit the rumor. Even if it serves only to verify a problem, the rumor provides a basis for making plans to confront the troubling situation.

In other words, for positive rumors the alleviation of discomfort may be a reinforcement of an expected outcome of a rumor. The uneasiness of "getting one's hopes up only to be later disappointed" is alleviated. For example, if a faculty member hears that the strike will not occur and has confidence in the truth of this rumor, the rumor may be transmitted to alleviate stress. Feedback

10

from others that support the belief tends to reassure and minimize the discomfort brought on by uncertainty and anxiety. For negative rumors, the alleviation of discomfort may come in the form of a plan to cope with the ramifications of the outcome of the rumor. For example, if an individual has confidence in a rumor that states that there will be a strike, the person may transmit the rumor in order to assess what to do in case of a strike.

Rumors can also provide social sanctions for those passing them to say negative things about others (Knapp, 1944). If one is sure of the truth of a rumor, the discomfort stemming from the situation will be alleviated and the usual social taboos will be less likely to come into play. In this study, 25 percent of all negative rumors (20 percent of all rumors) were hostile, which is to say that they assigned the blame for an imminent strike to the president of the university or the administration. This is analogous to a worker who dislikes a manager saying hostile things about the manager through rumors, which is a normatively acceptable form of disparagement during a stressful situation. In this way, rumors may have a purging effect.

Further investigation is warranted to see if the findings of this study can be generalized in other naturalistic settings. With reports of rumors continuing to proliferate recently in the stock market (Wiggins, 1985) and the business world (Koenig, 1985), additional research on the topic is needed.

References

Allport, G. W., & Postman, L. (1947). The psychology of rumor. New York: Holt, Rinehart & Winston.

Allport, G. W., & Lepkin, M. (1945). Wartime rumors of waste and special privilege: Why some people believe them. Journal of Abnormal and Social Psychology, 40, 3-36.

Jaeger, M. E., Anthony, S., & Rosnow, R. L. (1980). Who hears what from whom and with what effect: A study of rumor. Personality and Social Psychology Bulletin, 6, 473-478.

Knapp, R. H. (1944). A psychology of rumor. Public Opinion Quarterly, 8, 22-37.

Koenig, F. (1985). Rumor in the marketplace: The social psychology of commercial hearsay. Dover, MA: Auburn House.

Nkpa, N. K. U. (1975). Rumormongering in war time. Public Opinion Quarterly, 96, 27-35.

Prasad, J. (1935). The psychology of rumor: A study relating to the great Indian earthquake of 1934. British Journal of Psychology, 26, 1-15.

Rosenthal, R., & Rosnow, R. L. (1985). Contrast analysis: Focused comparisons in the analysis of variance. Cambridge, England: Cambridge University Press.

Rosnow, R. L. (1980). Psychology of rumor reconsidered. Psychological Bulletin, 87, 578-591.

Wiggins, P. H. (1985, February 14). Safeway rise and rumors. The New York Times.

Appendix: Statistical Computations

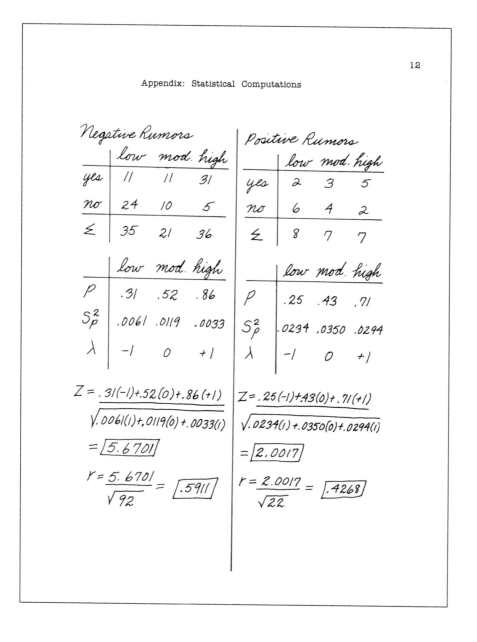

Negative Rumors

	low	mod.	high
yes	11	11	31
no	24	10	5
Σ	35	21	36

	low	mod.	high
P	.31	.52	.86
S_p^2	.0061	.0119	.0033
λ	-1	0	$+1$

$$Z = \frac{.31(-1) + .52(0) + .86(+1)}{\sqrt{.0061(1) + .0119(0) + .0033(1)}}$$

$$= \boxed{5.6701}$$

$$r = \frac{5.6701}{\sqrt{92}} = \boxed{.5911}$$

Positive Rumors

	low	mod.	high
yes	2	3	5
no	6	4	2
Σ	8	7	7

	low	mod.	high
P	.25	.43	.71
S_p^2	.0234	.0350	.0294
λ	-1	0	$+1$

$$Z = \frac{.25(-1) + .43(0) + .71(+1)}{\sqrt{.0234(1) + .0350(0) + .0294(1)}}$$

$$= \boxed{2.0017}$$

$$r = \frac{2.0017}{\sqrt{22}} = \boxed{.4268}$$

Index

DATE DUE

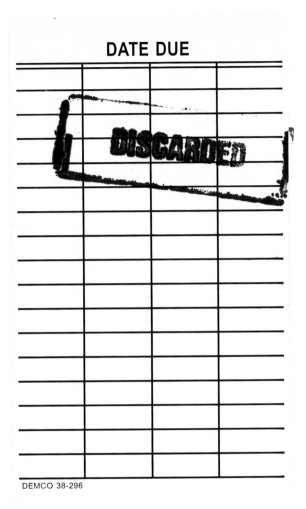